Simple
Killing Complexity for a Lean and Agile Organization

Simple
Killing Complexity for a Lean and Agile Organization

Barry Cross

CRC Press
Taylor & Francis Group
Boca Raton London New York

CRC Press is an imprint of the
Taylor & Francis Group, an **informa** business

A PRODUCTIVITY PRESS BOOK

CRC Press
Taylor & Francis Group
6000 Broken Sound Parkway NW, Suite 300
Boca Raton, FL 33487-2742

© 2017 by Taylor & Francis Group, LLC
CRC Press is an imprint of Taylor & Francis Group, an Informa business

No claim to original U.S. Government works

Printed on acid-free paper

International Standard Book Number-13: 978-1-138-71343-7 (Hardback)
International Standard Book Number-13: 978-1-3151-9875-0 (eBook)

Library of Congress Cataloging-in-Publication Data

Names: Cross, Barry L., author.
Title: Simple : killing complexity for a lean and agile organization / Barry Cross.
Description: Boca Raton, FL : CRC Press, 2017. | Includes bibliographical references and index.
Identifiers: LCCN 2016050455 | ISBN 9781138713437 (hardback : alk. paper)
Subjects: LCSH: Organizational change. | Organizational behavior. | Organizational effectiveness.
Classification: LCC HD58.8 .C755 2017 | DDC 658.4/06--dc23
LC record available at https://lccn.loc.gov/2016050455

Visit the Taylor & Francis Web site at
http://www.taylorandfrancis.com

and the CRC Press Web site at
http://www.crcpress.com

Contents

List of Figures

Acknowledgments

A number of people and organizations played key roles in the development and writing of this book, knowingly or otherwise, and all have my sincere gratitude.

My readers—Cheryl and David Green, Katrina Cross—your input, suggestions, sharp eyes, and comments were invaluable. Many of your ideas led to further development throughout the book. Thank you!

You may note that my approach to illustrations have been punched up a bit from what was published in *Lean Innovation*. All credit here goes to my new graphic artist, Rosey Li. Thanks Rosey! Check out her work at www.roseyli.com.

There are two CEOs that I have known for years and whose work is the embodiment of what I have created here with *Simple*. Darren Dalgleish is a longtime friend and former coworker, and now heads up St. Lawrence Parks Commission (SLPC) in Ontario, Canada. What he and his team have done over the past five years in turning around SLPC, eliminating a generation of complexity, and focusing on creating customer value is nothing short of remarkable. He has taken a business model designed around the summer tourist season and extended it to virtually the full calendar, preserving SLPC's central themes along the way.

Carrie Gregoire is the CEO of Quinte First Credit Union, which was really a small player with an identity crisis in banking, behaving much like its far larger peers when she took over the organization. She has been relentless in her vision of identifying and understanding her core customers (or members), and has single-handedly driven the business to operate as a members-first entity. Not a bank!

Thank you to all my students, leadership program participants, and clients over the years, for supporting and reinforcing my ideas around the theme of simplicity and agility in all organizations. Those discussions, programs, and situations continue to help us all understand and appreciate the concept of speed, regardless of our industry.

My thanks again to my colleagues, the faculty, staff, and administration at Queen's University's Smith School of Business, for the opportunity to work in such a creative environment. You are a sounding board, platform, and catalyst. Here is to another 10 years.

To Michael Sinocchi, Alexandria Gryder, and the team at Productivity Press—thank you for your faith in me and this project. You were terrific! Any mistakes in the book are once again the sole domain of the author.

Finally, thank you most of all to Katrina, Regan, and Declan—you are my inspiration, true north, and center of the known universe.

Introduction

This is a book about speed, agility, and execution, strategic priorities that have been evolving for our organizations over the last 10 years. Customers demand everything faster, having tasted overnight, free delivery from Amazon, and often customized to their needs. Philanthropists want to put their money to work, demanding greater accountability and *benefit* from charities they support. Students and employers want more flexible scheduling and a variety of delivery options, with programming evolving almost daily in colleges and universities. All the while, employees remain mired in bureaucracy, policies, and procedures preventing them from focusing on areas of the operation where they can create true value.

Product and service life cycles are shortening, perhaps more quickly than we realize. What we are doing today as an organization will likely be made obsolete far earlier than anticipated when that offering was introduced to our strategy. Disrupters will come from outside our industry, like Tesla and Google to the automotive market, Uber to taxis, and Netflix to television programming. Can you see past the calm seas to these threats forming just beyond your horizon?

We understand the world has changed, yet the problems and barriers associated with working faster often feel insurmountable to the firm, including challenges such as

- Legacy structures, policies, and processes within our firms.
- Without controls, *fast* leads to errors and mistakes, and justifiably, our customers and regulatory system are very intolerant of those mistakes.
- Our culture may be more cautious, pondering, and as a result, appear lethargic.
- Complexity slows us down and often prevents us from knowing precisely where to focus our attention and energy.
- And most often, we simply don't know where to start.

Simple: Killing Complexity for a Lean and Agile Organization is about understanding those challenges, however significant, and resolving what I refer to as the barriers to agility in the interest of enabling the firm to begin to really *move*. The book is about driving change and creating opportunities where they are currently hidden, and focusing on what matters most to you and your organization right now. My approach is aligned to your customer; we all have customers we need to think about, know, and understand to a much greater degree. Simplicity begins with an ability to understand who those customers are, and what they want from our firm. The lessons apply to all operations, from traditional businesses to health care, government, not-for-profits, and education.

A bit about terminology. *Simple*, in this case, is by no means an indication of intended work. Driving this kind of change in your business will not be simple or easy, and the last thing I am trying to do is insult the organization's leadership by saying, "Hey, it's simple!" *Simple* is a reflection of the outcome of this effort: a customer-focused, aligned organization that understands its goals and priorities, with straightforward, tested, and proven techniques to deliver ongoing value, changes that cause ripples across the whole firm. As we reduce and eliminate the complexity in our processes, planning and execution, we simplify our perspective; objectives become clearer, challenges easier to identify, and employees better able to align their own work in support of the organization's strategy.

Agile is about speed, how quickly we react, move, and operate as a team. This is about jettisoning the baggage and teaching the metaphorical elephant to dance, in concert with the other dancers on the floor. The book is not about the agile project management methodology, with its scrums and sprints, although those familiar with that system may see some philosophical and operational overlap.

Many an executive has admired the agile behavior demonstrated by start-ups, the get-it-done mentality without worry for process or what human resources would think. Some of these same executives are visiting start-up operations in Silicon Valley and elsewhere, hoping some of that magic will rub off. They bring back the open-concept office layouts, juice bars, and flexible wardrobes, and nothing really changes.*

Start-ups think differently. For them, it's about survival, and only doing what is absolutely necessary right now. They don't have the time or money or often the inclination to build complicated processes or staff up a human

---

* In the same fashion, companies have been visiting and touring Toyota for years, and Toyota, for the most part, is happy to have them. Toyota knows that the visitors may pick up an operating tip or two, but no real competitive advantages will be threatened because Toyota *thinks differently* than its competition, and is pretty confident that none of these visiting executives will master the ability to read minds.

resources department. If something doesn't make sense right now, *they don't do it*. This is a key agile concept we can all adopt from a start-up organization. Strategy is often described as deciding not only what to do, but also what not to do. An *agile* mindset within the firm operates the same way, but extends it beyond strategy to all levels of our operations. This is where things simplify, and clarity of purpose and focus give us new abilities within our business.

Keep in mind that this is going to take time and sustained effort and will. Some of the things I talk about in the book will be low-hanging fruit and you will be able to make improvements immediately. In many cases, however, you need to appreciate the time it will take, the momentum you need to build, and the alignment you must achieve in order to drive sustainable change. You can't rush a turnaround.

This is my third book. Those of you who have been with me through all three will recognize the style and writing; I tend to write like I talk. Some have told me that it is a very approachable and readable style. Others, I'm sure, think I'm kind of simple myself, perhaps lacking in refinement or sophistication. I am okay with that. I have built in my own version of humor in many places, including the stories, anecdotes, and most often, the footnotes.

A new feature in this book is what I call "One Last Story." I firmly believe in the idea of starting and ending with a story, with any theory tucked firmly in the middle. I like these stories, so I've punched them up a bit with a snappy heading. They are quick, all have a message related to the content of that chapter, some are fun, and they are all true (I swear, even the GoPro™ story), although the Mexican blankets story may have been embellished a bit.

I hope you enjoy the book.

1

Who Is Your Customer?

It's not the big beating the small anymore. It's the fast beating the slow.

Rupert Murdoch

Why are you in business? What is the singular purpose for which you get up in the morning? Who is your most important customer, and what do they want from your organization? Can you answer those questions, truthfully, honestly? Could others, at the top level of the firm, respond appropriately?

Companies compete in an increasingly complex world; this won't surprise you. What surprises many is that we really don't compete all that well. Many industries wallow in mediocrity, competing on price while customers struggle to find a company that truly understands service. Businesses are disappearing faster than ever before, with publicly traded firms now facing 1 in 3 odds of being delisted in the next five years.[1] Firms fail to hit goals and objectives, yet in many cases, executives in these firms earn bonuses at year-end and are not held accountable for any lack of execution.

Organizations are not intentionally reckless, ignoring customers or casually failing to get things done. I believe that in many cases, they struggle to appreciate what really matters as they both manage day-to-day operations and develop priorities for tomorrow. The complexities of managing in today's world both obscure decision making and layer on challenges that bog an organization down, preventing leadership from understanding what their customers want.

Municipalities are putting bylaws in place in the interest of safety, which ultimately protect taxi companies driving 20-year-old vehicles and prevent innovators like Uber from offering local citizens an alternative. Waiting lines for health care analysis, such as an MRI, can extend to months, while the condition requiring that exam in the first place often gets worse. The demand for improved accuracy with officiating in professional sports led to the adoption of after-the-play review by umpires, referees, and even officials located in other cities behind computer screens, reviews that can take 5–10 minutes to conclude in many circumstances, as the officials strive to get the call "right." These organizations are not intentionally doing a poor job, yet they appear unaware or have forgotten what matters most, and implemented complexity in the form of policies, procedures, or processes that slow the system down, creating a negative experience for the end customer, user, or viewer.

At the same time, other organizations excel.

- Virginia Mason Medical Center, a private, not-for-profit hospital, launched a Lean campaign in 2002, studying the Toyota Production System in an effort to improve patient safety and overall health care. As part of the initiative, they were able to virtually eliminate all waiting rooms and patient queuing around the hospital, while saving the center more than $12 million.
- A decade ago, Passport Canada overhauled its information technology (IT) systems and passport application process, resulting in a reduction in time to approve a passport renewal from 6 weeks to roughly 10 days. Resources saved within this initiative were then applied to increasing the security of the Canadian passport system.
- St. Lawrence Parks Commission, the operator of a number of historical and tourist sites in eastern Ontario, was able to reduce and virtually eliminate its reliance on government funding over a period of five years by implementing a customer focus and introducing appealing new products and attractions, attracting tens of thousands of new visitors annually.
- Maple Leaf Foods completed a seven-year Lean campaign that streamlined manufacturing processes, refreshed product portfolios, and eliminated costly downtime in production line conversions.
- In 2014, Tim Horton's, the Canadian icon of coffee and donuts, cleared numerous products from its menu, freeing up resources to focus on more impactful offerings.

What would it take for your organization to transform in this manner, to drive change and become truly agile? Companies exist in an increasingly complex and complicated world, making it all the more important to monitor that complexity in the pursuit of simpler methods. Failure will happen; our strategy will need to adapt and evolve, reacting to new and changing customer needs. An agile mindset enables that nimble evolution, builds in urgency, and keeps us focused; a slow and sluggish bureaucratic approach will lead to extinction.

Here is that question again: Who is your customer, and what do they want? Can you identify your organization's customers, especially its best customers? Do we speak in that type of language around the boardroom table?

In 1954, behavioral academic Gregory Stone published his seminal research identifying four types of consumers: *personalizing, convenience, ethical,* and *economizing.* Think about some of your recent service experiences as a consumer, and try to identify which "type" you are. For most of us, the answer is, it depends. For clothing or electronics, you likely choose items that identify with your lifestyle, and personalize the experience. When looking for something simple like shampoo or toothpaste, it might be about convenience (which store is closest?) or cost (what else do I need at Wal-Mart?).

Retailers and many service providers can be identified by applying Stone's terminology. Wal-Mart would be described as appealing to economizing customers, but given the number of stores in the chain, one could also suggest that they are a convenience retailer, with locations near most of the population. Amazon would also be convenience, in that we shop from the comfort of our den, living room, or kitchen. Their broad selection and delivery options may also support a nod toward personalization.

It is interesting that even 60 years later, Stone's customer categorizations, for the most part, still stand. More importantly, organizations that ignore or fail to recognize who their customers really are do so at their peril. When working with students and executives on strategy or innovation, I look at two fundamental questions: *Who is your customer,* and *what does that customer really want?* Knowing who your customer is today enables operations and drives a successful customer experience. Understanding tomorrow's customers sets the table for effective innovation.

Let's look at a couple recent examples.

The first is McDonald's, which has struggled in recent years with an expanding menu, slower service, and numerous failed product launches. In 2013, McDonald's launched "Mighty Wings" at 14,000 of its locations across the United States. Eight weeks later, there remained 10 million pounds of leftover wings in inventory as the product flopped (flapped?) with customers.[2] The problem wasn't the wing itself—customers actually loved the big, meaty wing. Priced at a dollar each, however, the issue was cost—the wings were too expensive for a McDonald's patron.

Some of us eat at McDonald's periodically, some don't, but over the years, most of us have dined under the golden arches at one time or another. With more than 7% of the U.S. market by number of restaurants, McDonald's is still almost three times the size of its nearest competitor. Innovation blunders like Mighty Wings don't help the cause, so let's drill down a bit. In Stone's language, who are the typical McDonald's customers? *Convenience*, sure. With so many locations, long hours, and generally fast service, we can get in and out in a hurry when we are hungry. Some might also say *economizing*, in that "dinner out" runs under $10 per person, less than most sit-down establishments. *Personalizing* and *ethical* don't really enter the discussion when we talk about McDonald's, and it could even be argued that some of McDonald's recent struggles are a result of being less convenient (larger menus slow down service) and less economizing, to the point where traditional McDonald's customers are growing weary.

What concerns me the most is that McDonald's doesn't seem to be learning from its mistakes. Now on its third CEO in as many years, it is innovating again, and once more neglecting who its customers are and what they truly want. In 2015, McDonald's launched the "Create Your Taste" menu as a trial at select New York locations.[3] With a nice bit of technology, the restaurant installed large touch screens where patrons enter their own orders, giving the customers control over the process. Customers select their bun or bread, meat, toppings, and sauces. Sounds great, right? Perhaps not, as two challenges quickly emerged. First is speed—the customer-driven order process slows down the ordering process on a menu that already includes more than 100 items, especially in groups or families who crowd around the screen asking each other, "What are you having?" Initial data indicates that orders from the Create Your Taste menu take 10 minutes or more to arrive, perhaps as a result of the additional complexity being introduced in a very standardized kitchen environment. Second, and more importantly, is cost, with meals from this new menu typically totaling $12. While there are many people (myself included) who will pay $12 for a good burger or sandwich, I do not believe McDonald's will attract this kind of customer. A premium burger like that is a personalizing experience, and personalizing customers remain the domain of the roadhouse or gourmet burger shop. Innovations that do not align with customers will fail, and for me, this means back to the drawing board.

Another example comes from Elon Musk's garage at Tesla, which, on the surface, seems very exciting. Musk recently announced the introduction of a new Tesla SUV, the Model X. This is a good-looking, small SUV typical of Tesla's styling and features, which launched in 2016. The Model X debuts with a sexy set of "falcon-wing" doors on the back of the vehicle, an attractive styling feature that apparently eases access to the rear-seating compartment. Kudos to the designers for not using the term *gull-wing doors* from the 1980s—gulls are not sexy.

Think back now to our shaping questions for strategy and innovation: *Who is the customer*, and *what do they want*? Who is a Tesla customer? We can say they are personalizing (anyone willing to pay $130,000 for a car is looking for something particular), and likely ethical, given Tesla's electric power plant and the elimination of the side effects of a combustion engine.

So what is the problem, you ask. Well, let's look at this from another angle. Who are SUV customers? We know they are just about any age, but are active, and generally haul a lot of "stuff," from golf clubs to baby and toddler gear (aka the luggage club), to skis, bikes, and paddleboards. What do those SUV customers want? They want the storage space, performance, and utility to get them and their gear where they are going. On the Model X, I believe the practical needs of the SUV customer trump the styling needs of the Tesla customer. The falcon-wing doors look great, but how do I put a roof rack on the truck? How do I put stuff on that roof rack with the doors open? Any of you who have done this appreciate that you need to open the front and rear doors to install the racks, ski boxes, or other gear on the roof. You stand on the door liner and load up. You could, in theory, keep the rear doors closed and use a stepladder to install and load the roof system in the comfort of your garage, but the fancy doors pretty much mean you need to bring that stepladder with you to unload at the ski hill. Worse yet, with a roof rack installed, you have to leave the kids at home—the back doors won't open with the ski box on top.

Most of us give full credit to Musk and his minions for their creativity and innovation. From PayPal to Tesla to his Gigafactory battery plant to Space X and others, Musk continues to push the envelope and drive products and services in new directions. In this case, however, in what we might refer to as a rare miss, the team forgot about the customer. SUV customers want a roof, and the roof on the Model X is not accessible. An important tenant of innovation is that it is okay to fail—time for Tesla to learn from this failure and redesign the fancy rear doors to a traditional, or least functional, design.

Think about your innovation process. Is the team thinking about your customers? What do these customers want? Most importantly, what will they want next year? Then, how will you deliver? Failure to take these questions into account will lead to failed innovations like Mighty Wings and falcon wings, and others that are likely to underperform through a misalignment to customer needs and tastes.

Let us consider two other examples where the company does a very good job of understanding the needs of its customer. For the first example, think about appetizers. Many enjoy a good dip before a meal with friends or family, and one dip or appetizer that really draws a crowd is Tex-Mex style, with grated cheese, sour cream, guacamole, tomatoes, and so forth, arranged in multiple layers. There is an art to preparing these dips that is typically only rivaled by the science in consuming them. The problem? The crackers and nacho chips we use to load up the dip often fracture under the burden of our load, or during the actual scooping process.

We then try to delicately and hygienically remove the scraps of our chip and resume the process of acquiring the tasty sample we were pursuing in the first place. You've been there too, right? Many of you have seen the solution to this dilemma as well, courtesy of our friends at Tostitos and their Scoops™ nacho chip. This is perhaps the best example of the perfect product in the consumer space, and certainly without peer in the chip and dip category. The physicists and engineers at Tostitos watched the behavior of their customers around kitchens, food islands, living rooms, and restaurants everywhere—one can only imagine their commitment and dedication as they went to Super Bowl™ parties, pub nights, and 50th birthday celebrations everywhere, watching both the execution of a good dipping stroke and the anguish of yet another broken chip as they gathered their market and customer data. The output of said research is the bowl-shaped nacho chip with scalloped edges; the bowl and the edge effects create a far stronger structure, and the perfect size scoop, that results in the ultimate delivery vehicle for your dip of choice. No more breakage, no more spillage; focus on the game!

Now, we can have some fun talking about Scoops and recreational dipping, but without an appreciation of the customers' snacking experience and needs, that product innovation wouldn't have happened, and we would all still be fishing broken chips out of our dip. Who is our customer, and what do they want?

Keeping with our food theme for another moment, my next example arrived courtesy of our daughter Regan while we were visiting her during her first year of university. She had discovered the local outpost of the Menchie's frozen yogurt chain.* Think of all the dessert bars, ice cream chains, and the like that you have encountered over the years. Like me, you have likely tried sundaes, banana splits, cones (with and without dip), and their endless brands and varieties. Most are priced in the $3–$5 range. If this were your store, then, how would you differentiate? How would you get people to pay even more, and in fact, line up for the experience? The answer—let them build it.

Menchie's is a chain of 300+ stores,† with a modest goal of hitting 2000 locations within 20 years. I think they will do it. Their secret is to give the customer control, and the concept is brilliant in its simplicity. Customers enter the store and select the bowl or cone of their choice. The customers then proceed to choose their flavor of frozen yogurt and toppings from the myriad choices along two buffet-style bars. How does Menchie's determine how much to charge for the custom-made sundae? They weigh your creation at checkout. Customers pay by the pound (in a nasty case of *cause and effect*, if I do say so).

This service concept works because the customer has control, and subconsciously or consciously, we all want more control over our service experience, and your degree of satisfaction goes up in direct correlation to your control. At Menchie's, like any buffet, the consumer decides what they want and how much to take, and they prepare the sundae themselves— no surprises, no hygiene issues, and no bad decision risk associated with ordering the wrong dessert.

A primary theme for this book is the idea of knowing your customer. Sadly, surprisingly few organizations have a clear appreciation of who their best customers are. In fact, when discussing this idea with leadership teams in numerous industries, many an executive has gently pushed back, stating, "Barry, our industry is a bit different. We don't actually have customers we identify that way."

This is a significant problem for those organizations, yet many remain unaware of the impact of that ignorance. Think about value for a moment. The creation and delivery of value is the foundation of Lean activities everywhere. Lean programs, therefore, focus on complexity and the

---

* Despite all this talk of food, our family is actually quite healthy. Honest.
† As of 2015.

reduction of activities that don't create value, enabling more resources around the firm to concentrate on delivering more value. This deserves repeating: Lean is about reducing waste in the organization, so that more resources can focus on work that matters. Now, who decides what products, services, or processes around the firm truly have value? Ultimately, the customer.

For those organizations, then, who do not have a clear appreciation of who their core customers are, how do they determine what activities within the firm create value? The answer is, they often can't. The output of this lack of customer clarity for these firms typically manifests itself in the form of unnecessary product proliferation (as noted earlier with McDonald's), misguided innovation (Tesla's falcon-wing doors on the Model X), cluttered service structures, or issues within their business processes. Collectively, these issues bog a firm down, reducing its agility and ability to drive customer enthusiasm.

One of the outputs of our connected society is a lack of patience within our markets. Customers have access to so much information, and answers to any question that may come up, that solutions to many of life's challenges have become almost instantaneous. Have a question? *Google* it! Need a restaurant? Check *TripAdvisor* and call for a reservation. Last night's scores? Open your app or check the ESPN or TSN website. Quarterly or even more frequent analyst calls mean management in many organizations is so focused on the short term that committing resources to innovation or other longer-term initiatives can be a challenge. Sports franchises are expected to perform right now as well; coaches and managers with winning records or even a run at the championship the season prior are fired three months into this season if the team seems to be underperforming. Everything is *now*, which by extension means that people seem to have less patience than ever before. Organizations that can't compete on speed, regardless of their field, will lag; management will be replaced, new strategies developed, and operations tuned until pace and agility are key indicators.

There are a number of potential outcomes for an enterprise that knows its customers, as enhanced service experience or improved product design are both within reach. Cost reduction through the elimination of waste is enabled. Differentiation in numerous ways becomes possible. My goal, however, through the following 50,000 or so words, is to focus on speed and agility by reducing the complexity within your business.

Our foundational questions again—*who is your customer*, and *what do they want*? For most of our organizations, regardless of what type of business we run, we can answer the second question the same way. Whether we are a product company or a service organization, for profit or not, government agency or school board or military—your customers are buying your execution, your ability to make things happen and get things done. That is the primary reason they walk in the door every day. Satisfying today's customers, then, is the domain of your operations, and the plan we establish to map out how those customers will be satisfied is your operations strategy. Your operations strategy is subordinate to your overall organizational strategy, in that it tends to focus on the now and near future, while the broader strategy also considers customers, operations, and technologies several years down the line, depending on the type of business you operate. In a broader sense, then, we need an understanding and appreciation of not only who our customers are today, but who they will be in 3 years, 5 years, or 10 years. As we will see in subsequent chapters, the concept of our customer is central to strategy discussions, Lean, innovation, and execution in and around the firm.

These are not new concepts, but I believe my presentation of them in this manner enables a simpler, clearer perception of the need for alignment between understanding our customer and the driving purpose of our firm. Here are a few more examples to help solidify the idea.

Sandra Vandermerwe and Juan Rada pioneered the idea of servitization in 1988 in their work "Servitization of Business: Adding Value by Adding Service."[4] *Servitization*, as they defined it almost 30 years ago, is the application of service operations in a product-based business to drive additional customer enthusiasm.

Think about the service department at your Lexus dealership, the Apple store, or the OnStar service on your General Motors vehicle. Those services, when operating well, enhance your enjoyment and perception of the vehicle or electronics product you own.

In their research, Vandermerwe and Rada examine a number of firms, including Xerox and its copier business. Over the years, Xerox's concept of who its customer was evolved from the person in the purchasing department who bought or leased the copier to the users and the admin responsible for managing the copier. Xerox developed the ability to monitor the performance of the copier remotely, and then call that customer to advise if a door was open, the copier was out of paper, or other issues. Uptime on the copiers increased, and with that, so did customer appreciation, while actual maintenance and service calls went down.*

Amazon took a similar servitization approach with the Kindle as the e-reader market evolved over the last 15 years.[5] Sony and other manufacturers produced arguably superior products, with improved battery life, readability, weight, and handling, but really had no ability to influence the utility of their e-readers. That is, potential e-reader customers wanted more and easier access to books, something Sony and the others had little control over. Amazon, on the other hand, obviously carried significant weight with publishers and content providers, and could not only increase the availability of electronic media, but also ensure it was published in the Kindle format. Thus, Kindle buyers had access to the most titles, and Kindle quickly became the number one e-reader on the market.

Sears, the once dominant retailer, has struggled now for years to find its place in a world ruled by the likes of Wal-Mart, Costco, and Amazon. Who are Sears customers? With utter and undying respect to this group, we think of Sears shoppers as our parents, in-laws, and other seniors and baby boomers. These are the people who have stuck with Sears as the retail universe shifted dramatically over the last 25 years. Can an organization build an enduring retail strategy with that customer category? Possibly, but as of 2016, that has not been Sears's strategy, and existing enthusiasm among that demographic is essentially by default. Sears is not a one-stop shopping destination for this group, but it does offer personal and home fashion, hardware, furniture, appliances and electronics, and other products with service that is easy and familiar.

Some have criticized Sears as having an identity crisis—"Who goes to a store to buy a wrench, a blouse and a toaster oven?"[6] Well, um, Target, Wal-Mart, Costco, and others all offer the same product diversity and do quite well, thank you. I do not buy the "identity crisis" argument. I do, however, contend that the customer group currently loyal to Sears has less use for things like hardware. My father, for example, got rid of most of his tools years ago, other than the basics, and now hires someone when something more significant needs to be done around the house.

Sears needs to decide who its customers are, and will be, and align its operating strategy to support those customers. If that segment happens to be seniors, so be it! Offer products and services those people want to buy.

---

* Ironically, what Xerox struggled with was how to make this improved service more visible to the customer so that the customer ultimately appreciated what they were getting with a Xerox copier.

Provide shuttles and transportation, make the stores more accessible, and provide seating. Make the font size larger on price tags and product information, and send monthly bills and statements by mail with no additional charge if customers opt in that direction.

Sears has sold or closed hundreds of locations in recent years as volumes and sales plummet across the chain. Some reports indicate it is returning to its catalog roots, with a focus on e-commerce and online shopping,[7] while others indicate that Sears is focusing on a customer known as "Amy," a middle-aged, middle-class woman with children and a minivan. Both retail segments are crowded already, so it remains to be seen how successful they will be in the future. I honestly wish them well—my part-time job in high school was at the local Sears store where I did everything from working the retail floor to stocking shelves in the warehouse to riding shotgun on the delivery truck.

A significant part of our discussion so far has surrounded the idea of knowing your customer. Well, how do we do that? In some cases, the customer may be relatively obvious. At McDonald's and Wal-Mart, for example, the customer is focused on economizing and convenience, to apply Stone's terminology again. In other organizations, knowing your customer takes a bit more work.

When the Georgia Aquarium in Atlanta opened in 2005, customers lined up at the door, initially in a situation of "we built it and they came," to play on *Field of Dreams.* After a few years, however, the novelty of the world's biggest indoor aquarium wore off and crowds thinned. Georgia Aquarium leadership talked to other similar operations and found that this was an industry-wide problem.*

Carey Rountree, the aquarium's senior vice president of sales and marketing, reevaluated the situation, however, with a fresh look at their customer base. With the help of a Georgia State University expert, V. Kumar (VK to his friends, colleagues, and students), Rountree developed a new marketing strategy with the goal of not just attracting more customers, but also attracting the "right" customers. Once the aquarium knew who those people were, it could design a marketing plan tailored to their interests, media, and behaviors. VK's team and Rountree started by determining which zip codes the top seasons' pass holders and net spenders resided

---

* I had a chance to tour the facilities in 2014, and the experience is still exceptional, with different exhibits teeming with marine life from literally around the world. As an avid scuba diver, to be able to get up close and personal with some of these animals without the need for complicated travel, boats, and equipment was a real pleasure.

in (i.e., returning guests who obviously aligned well with the aquarium's service proposition), and the zip codes that held the most "regular" or one-time visitors. The team found 40 zip codes that were on both lists, and from there, they were able to create a profile of the aquarium's most important customers—married with children under the age of 14, household income of $50,000 or more, and an affinity for entertainment outside the home. That knowledge allowed them to be much more specific in both the geographic spend and how the message was delivered within their marketing budget.[8] Any of you with a sales and marketing background can appreciate the value of that knowledge, and the ability to be much more specific and target your message, rather than applying a broader shotgun approach.

It is difficult to overemphasize the importance of a clear understanding of who your customer is and what attracts them. In the realm of sports, and more specifically baseball, franchises and owners make money from the fans (tickets, merchandise, food, and beverage) and from the team's success (broadcast royalties, endorsements, and an increase in the aforementioned tickets, merchandise, etc.). While many teams see cyclicality to their financial and playing field success, what has been consistent over a number of years has been the drop in viewership for televised baseball broadcasts.[9] Owners and executives could speculate that customers are disappearing, leaving the sport. Digging further, however, we note that the number of fans attending actual games in stadiums has increased by almost 50% over the last 20 years. In the first two weeks of the 2015 season alone, 3 million fans attended games in person, more than any similar time frame in a prior season.

Who are these new customers, then? Saying they are baseball fans alone would be somewhat narrow in focus. The environment the games are played in has changed significantly over the last 25 years. In fact, only 6 of the 30 stadiums in baseball were constructed before 1989, including the iconic Fenway Park in Boston in 1912 and Wrigley Field in Chicago in 1914. The new stadiums are different, with water effects, retractable roofs, more and better corporate boxes, larger Jumbotrons, fireworks, and unrestricted lines of sight. New stadiums boast some of the best fan food, beverages, and entertainment ever, and owners are capitalizing on this and ticket prices reflect it. Ultimately, these fans remain baseball fans, but they are more than that. These fans are also there for the experience— the sights, the sounds, the tastes, and yes, the event itself. Ownership and Major League Baseball recognized this with the opening of Oriole Park at

Camden Yards in Baltimore, with its asymmetric field, the incorporation of original brick architecture, and fan seating closer to the playing field. Camden Yards was immediately a hit, and its success created a new "retro" model of park design to capture more of these new baseball fans who were willing to pay more to be part of the experience.

Who are your customers? Do you know? Does the team even talk about the customer that way or ask the question? Firms like resort operator Sandals in the Caribbean make understanding their customers a priority (one resort general manager said to me, "Barry, you have no idea how much time we spend on *know the customer!*"), and that knowledge puts them at the top of their market year after year. Other firms do not think about the customer, and their lack of success and differentiation reflects that position, with products, services, and processes lacking alignment to customer value.

In the coming chapters, we will further our understanding and appreciation of our customer in the pursuit of what I call organizational agility; that is, the ability of the firm to react, move, and support what those customers want with increasing pace and ease. This is not new, but it is my firm belief that as much as any other competitive element, speed and time will be key in how we differentiate ourselves in our markets, especially in today's complex world. With that focus comes a reliance on understanding not only what our customers want, but also what they do not. As I have stated, this is the essence of Lean, and Lean is everywhere. There are books (and experts and gurus) on Lean start-ups, Lean engineering, Lean consulting, and even Lean accounting. In January 2016, Amazon produced more than 16,000 references with the word *Lean*.* Lean is out there, and has probably been overused at this point. My own perspective is that many applications and interpretations of the term *Lean* are wrong, incorrectly focused on cost cutting, head count reduction, and halfhearted efforts to do more with less. That is not what Lean is about. Lean is, and always has been, about the creation of value (what your customer wants and will pay for) and the reduction of waste and complexity (what your customer does not want to pay for).

While we will discuss and apply Lean concepts throughout the book, there is far more to the book than Lean. It is about the customer, and understanding that customer at the highest levels in the pursuit of an

---

* Including my own *Lean Innovation* (Taylor and Francis, 2012), relatively near the top, so I appreciate the irony here.

agile, responsive organization. At the end of the day, I believe that will create enthusiasm not only with your customers, but also within the workforce and other organizational stakeholders. The concepts apply not only to traditional businesses and corporations, but also to not-for-profits, government agencies, health care, education, and other fields. Indeed, many of our examples will relate to these fields, where some of the most significant opportunities exist.

ONE LAST STORY

This one supports my quest for good coffee. Back around 2004 or so, we purchased a Krups Aroma Control coffeemaker for around $100. This machine was recommended in someplace like *Consumer Reports*, *MoneySense*, or *Men's Health*. I do not remember where, but I read about it, bought it, and we loved it. In fact, my brother-in-law tried a cup and bought his own.

Let me tell you about the machine. It was easy to fill and had an on/off switch, a clear water-level indicator, and a glass-lined thermal carafe to keep the coffee warm (I get up an hour or so before my wife, Katrina, on weekends, and the coffee needs to stay hot without burning). There was nothing complicated about the machine, but it produced hot, flavorful coffee pot after pot, year after year, and then finally died in early 2014. I still miss that machine two years later.

Logically, we bought a new Krups, getting as close to the Aroma Control model as we could. The new machine was terrible. The coffee did not brew as hot, the pot dripped on the counter when we poured, the filling process was awkward, and the coffee had a metallic flavor. Frustrated, I banged around the online forums, read the reviews people submit on Amazon and elsewhere, and talked to buddies and coworkers (you are getting a sense of how important this is). Based on that research, we tried another brand, and then another, and then finally settled on a Cuisinart. Filling this one is still very awkward, and there is no external water-level indicator, but the coffee is hot and flavorful, and the machine itself is not unreasonably complicated.*

---

* A shout-out, by the way, to Keurig. We have one of their machines, and my sister-in-law owns and operates a store in Barrie, Ontario, that deals almost exclusively in Keurig's K-Cups, with something like 400 different cups available. What is the customer buying here? Personalization. Look them up at Personal Service Coffee.

The point of this story? What does the customer want? We (I) want an affordable, hot cup of coffee that tastes good. I wanted my old Krups again, but was denied. This seems like such a simple need as a customer, but so many of the offerings out there made the brewing process more complicated than it has to be, or messed with the flavor and temperature, or designed awkward filling systems in the interest of style. What better application for the keep it simple, stupid (KISS) theory is there than how you start the day?

REFERENCES

1. Reeves, M., Levin, S., and Ueda, D. The biology of corporate survival. *Harvard Business Review*, January–February 2016, p. 48.
2. Kowitt, B. Fallen arches: Can McDonald's get its mojo back? *Fortune*, November 2014.
3. Strauss, M. McDonald's launches 'Your Taste' menu. *Globe and Mail*, August 5, 2015.
4. Vandermerwe, S., and Rada, J. Servitization of business: Adding value by adding service. *European Management Journal*, Volume 6, Issue 4, Winter 1988, pp. 314–324.
5. Kim, W.C., and Mauborgne, R. Red ocean traps. *Harvard Business Review*, March 2015, p. 70.
6. Lutz, A. Four reasons Sears is headed straight for death. BusinessInsider.com, August 21, 2014.
7. Sears returns to catalogue. *Fortune*, December 22, 2014, p. 20.
8. Boosting demand in the "experience economy." *Harvard Business Review*, January–February 2015, pp. 24–26.
9. Matthews, C. Fields of greenbacks. *Fortune*, June 1, 2015, pp. 9–10.

2

Complexity and the Barriers to Agility

Cut through organization impediments and get some real work done.

Author's fortune cookie

A new retail category has emerged that is creating significant problems for the likes of Banana Republic and Eddie Bauer. The category is referred to as "fast fashion," and it is no surprise that retailers in this segment compete on speed and agility.

Traditional fashion retailers like Banana Republic (part of Gap Brands, along with Old Navy) order their merchandise up to a year in advance. Such a lead time allows suppliers to plan production, order fabrics and raw materials, and provide the best pricing back to Banana Republic and other retail customers. This has historically been a reliable system, as long as the retailer can accurately forecast customer demand. Underestimate demand, and customers leave unsatisfied, sales and profit are reduced, and market share suffers. Overestimate demand, and there are inventory costs, write-downs, and so forth. This is a simplistic view, but we get a sense of the risks and challenges associated with traditional supply issues; forecasting up to 12 months in advance with any accuracy would require a good sense of who the customer is and what their preferences are.

Alternatively, it means our styles and sizing are very middle of the road and not aligned with the needs of more fashion-forward customers.

For customers like me, this does not present a problem. I tend to buy quality clothing that will last a few years, and I am not really concerned with being on the cutting edge of fashion (no surprises here for my family). Unfortunately for me, I do not think that middle-aged professors are the focal point of a retailer's strategy. I expect that when they ask who their customers are, they are looking for a more significant demographic.

There are few bright lights at Gap Brands right now. Banana Republic sales were down 12% in the third quarter of 2015, and down 15% in October alone year over year. Share prices have dipped, and the head of Old Navy jumped ship to join Ralph Lauren. Most of these challenges are a result of the emergence of fast fashion with firms like Zara, H&M, and Forever 21.

Zara, for example, is not new, having been founded in 1975 and now operating more than 2000 stores in 88 countries. Its model, however, is nothing short of revolutionary in its industry. In most cases, Zara can design, produce, and stock an item in its stores in two to four weeks. It does this through a comprehensive operations strategy built on speed— Zara owns most of its supply chain, much of which is located in Europe. That control and proximity gives it the ability to do things like pulling an item that exhibits slow sales for a week or two and replacing it quickly with a new design. Materials used may not be of the highest quality, but Zara's customers do not expect to keep an item for years either. In fact, the combination of less costly material, a shorter supply chain, and substantially less inventory means comparable items from H&M, Zara, or Forever 21 can sell for less than half the price charged by traditional retailers.[1]

Zara's (and other fast-fashion retailers') speed and agility also means its product range can far exceed that of its competitors. Zara might produce 10,000–12,000 different items per year, compared with 3000 or 4000 in other chains.

Which came first, then? Did Zara and H&M react to customers demanding fashion-forward clothing at lower prices, greater selection, and more frequent turnover? Or, did they change the market and create a new category of customer? We would suspect the latter situation, and as often is the case with innovation and new business models, incumbents are left with their chins resting firmly on their chests, unsure of how to react in the face of declining sales and market share. Even traditional customers who are less fashion conscious appreciate the value in these stores—people will buy agility.

In another recent example, Kraft Foods has applied the simple, agile mindset with great success in its emerging markets. In the past, the company could be referred to as a lumbering giant, with dozens of product categories and 150 brands sold in 60 countries. Kraft's new president of developing markets, however, wanted the elephant to dance, and created a 5-10-10 strategy. That is, Kraft would focus on 5 strong categories, with 10 power brands in 10 key markets.[2] Other brands, categories, and markets were not necessarily shut down or abandoned, but resources were realigned within the firm to target the select few.*

This prioritization and focus worked, and six years into the strategy, Kraft's emerging market revenues have more than tripled, profits are up more than 50%, and cash flow has improved.

The lessons here are clear—agility relies on the ability within the firm to establish and communicate priorities and mandates with a foundation in value and what the customer truly wants. Zara reacts quickly to customer behavior and shopping patterns and can change over their entire inventory in a month. Kraft recognized that the increased complexity associated with focusing on 150 brands was bogging down their efforts in a rapidly evolving market, and opted for less complexity and the ability to react more quickly to key trends and customer needs. Less can be more when the customer is at the center of our strategy.

A complicated product mix, slow development process, and lethargic supply chain are just a few of the reasons organizations lack agility. These tend to be structural issues, where just as often, there are cultural or process issues that bog the firm down. Think of too many or unproductive meetings, ineffective communications, lots of talk but few decisions. In other cases, leadership may not feel they have the resources or expertise to do the things they believe are necessary, where without often realizing it, key resources are not aligned toward strategic priorities or what the customer wants.

I refer to these phenomena as *barriers to agility*, as summarized in Figure 2.1. Upon review, I believe most of us can identify with at least a few of these barriers. Kraft, for example, struggled with a perceived lack of resources until it narrowed its focus to the top 5 categories, 10 products, and 10 markets. With that clarity and alignment, Kraft suddenly had the resources it needed. Zara and H&M operate their supply chain, design, and merchandising strategies with a sense of urgency, with a clear focus on getting to those fashion-forward customers first.

---

* Those familiar with the organization will see similarities between Kraft's emerging market strategy and that of consumer goods firm Reckitt Benckiser. Reckitt refers to its priorities as power brands.

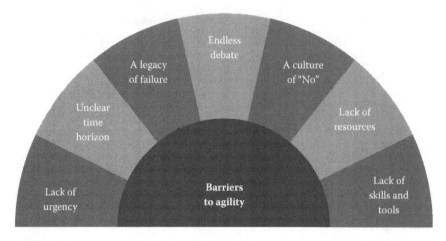

FIGURE 2.1
Barriers to agility.

BARRIERS TO AGILITY

Let's examine these barriers in more detail and consider how a particular barrier might manifest itself within our firm.

- *Lack of urgency*: Firms with a lack of urgency often struggle with short-term planning or the communication of priorities within that plan. Priorities and plans that have been established and conveyed to the team may not align with today's customers or their particular wants and needs. These firms may develop longer-term business plans, agreeing as a leadership team on the future direction of the organization, but the missing link is what we refer to here as an operating plan, or a clear vision of the activities in the next 12 months that will both satisfy the needs of today and lay the foundation for that longer-term agenda. I like to say that people can't do what they don't understand. In this case, the doing comes from an effective short-term plan and appropriate communication of that plan. "This is what we are doing, and more importantly, this is your role in that plan. We've studied it, and this is why it matters to the customer." We will spend more time on this in coming chapters, but it is essential to point out that *urgent* demand cannot trump *important* priorities. As Seth Godin once said, "Given the choice between urgent and important, urgent always wins." Effective prioritization enables people to react with both appropriateness and urgency in the right balance.

- *Unclear time horizon*: An unclear time horizon barrier typically goes hand in hand with a lack of urgency, and results from insufficient planning and communication. I distinguish between the two to highlight the necessity for an effective prioritization process within the organizational planning. Sometimes those events are presented in order of priority (first, second, and third), while more often, we get very specific with the due date of particular projects and events (second quarter next year; September 15 to align with the customer's launch date). Organizations that struggle in this area may have a number of important projects launching, say, next year, without a clear sense of which projects are more important than others, the appropriate cadence of projects to optimize resources, or an alignment of initiatives based on customer or market need. As a result, these firms toil with misspent resources and colliding projects and priorities and seem to be in fire-fighting mode more often than not.

- *Legacy of failure, and a culture of "no"*: These two are distinct barriers in some firms, and perhaps the same in others. Past failures lower the morale in a firm without a true innovation culture; where failure is part of the process, and often pursued in the interest of learning, refining an idea and evolving a new service or product go hand in hand. In the absence of innovation, failures breed cautious, risk-averse behavior, which can lead to additional policies, procedures, or processes to prevent such failures or issues from arising again. While this may be acceptable and appropriate in some cases, these processes often feel like additional stifling bureaucracy, slowing operations and response down.

  A "no" culture will also be familiar to many of us, especially when we hear things like, "That won't work here" or "We don't do it like that in this organization." These responses may have a foundation in the history of the organization, or perhaps the type of operation it is (e.g., health care, government, or education). This perspective is a barrier not only to agility, but also to innovation and general change within the industry.

- *Endless debate*: I work with a number of organizations that employ some of the brightest minds in their industry, including academia, banking, different government agencies, and companies in the technology sector. Anytime you gather intelligent, experienced, and intuitive people in a room, add a dose of hubris and perhaps a dash of arrogance, people with opinions want to offer them. Where this barrier devolves to an almost insurmountable situation is when we combine it with the lack of planning and alignment expressed in the urgency and timing barriers earlier. We like it when people contribute to the discussion—ultimately, that is why we hire and empower smart, capable people and hold the meeting in the first place. Without some connection to priorities, strategy, and customer needs, however, this discussion just goes on, often getting tabled "until we can circle back on this again."

- *Lack of resources, lack of skills and tools*: I will preface this section by stating that I have rarely gone into an organization and not been able to find the resources required to get the job done. In most of our organizations, we are not using those resources effectively, wasting people, time, space, and cash, often as a result of the previous barriers noted here. In these organizations, we have an insufficient focus on value creation. That is, we are not asking the tough questions related to the work that is consuming resources: Who is the customer of that process, and what do they really want? Why are we doing that? What is the agenda for the meeting you want me to attend? When was the last time anyone actually read this report or evaluated that data?

Collectively, this is the complexity—excess products, segments, categories, services, processes, policies, projects, regions, or whatever—that bogs us down. And, if we are honest about it, it resides in most of our organizations. Complexity consumes resources, often in the form of people completing work and tasks that serve no purpose or create no value for the firm or its customers. Why do we keep doing it that way? Well, we have always done it like that, or we are just following the procedure. Kill the complexity, free up resources, and begin to drive organizational agility.

For employees, complexity prevents them from focusing on the right areas, solving the right problems, or creating value for the right customers. It consumes their time, creates frustration, and wastes resources. For customers of these organizations, complexity creates confusion, anxiety, and bad decision risk.

Let's look back to our McDonald's example from Chapter 1 for more clarity. McDonald's current menu inside its restaurants has more than 120 items, all available every day, 365 days per year. In a fast-food environment, customers expect their meal to be prepared in just a few minutes, and be consistent from franchise to franchise, regardless of which city or part of the country we are in. Employees, therefore, should not have to think about what they are doing in the preparation of that meal. For most of those menu options, that is the case. Cooks prepare hundreds of Big Macs™, Quarter Pounders™, and Egg McMuffins™ every day. The processes in the kitchen, the equipment, and employee training allow for a consistent delivery of the product repeatedly and reliably. The more items on the menu, however, and the more likely there will be something ordered that a cook rarely prepares. McDonald's hires good people, but the majority are part-time employees, and turnover in many locations approaches 100%.* Newer, part-time employees are logically going to have more difficulty with rarely ordered menu items, affecting preparation time, food consistency, and quality as a result. For those employees, stress and anxiety increase as obscure items show up on their order screens.

For customers, extended menus take longer to peruse, potentially slowing down ordering lines during busy periods. Customer queues grow, customer frustration increases, and the environment itself suffers. Some customers, as a result, just "pick something" and may or may not be satisfied. Others suffer from bad decision risk anxiety, that buyer's remorse of worrying whether they will enjoy what they have ordered.

Such menu complexity is not the sole domain of fast-food restaurants. I have written and talked in the past about product proliferation in banks (20+ credit cards available from many financial institutions), smartphone manufacturers (11 different models of Blackberry), car companies (I contend that the Chevrolet and GMC pickup trucks are functionally identical, yet require millions of dollars of unique tooling and processes to produce), and even hot dogs (76 different flavors of wieners at Maple Leaf Foods in 2011). Rarely is this a case of "the more, the merrier." More often, such complexity results in slower internal processes, employee training issues, downtime, and waste, along with customer issues, such as slower ordering, anxiety, and bad decision risk.

In 2000, psychologists Sheena Iyengar and Mark Lepper published interesting results from their research involving customer choice.[3] In their study, on one day, shoppers at an upscale food market were presented

---

* Interestingly, turnover at McDonald's Canadian locations averages closer to 50%. In conversations with McDonald's executives, this is largely through a focus on skills development, goal sharing, and communication. Whatever the approach, it works—longer-tenured employees deliver better-quality product and service and are more responsive to change.

with a display table of 24 varieties of gourmet jam. On another day, shoppers saw a similar table, except that only six varieties of the jam were on display. The large display attracted more interest than the small one, and those who sampled the spreads received a coupon for $1 off any jam. But when the time came to purchase, people who saw the large display were only 10% as likely to buy as people who saw the small display.

This study and others have confirmed that not only can too much choice paralyze the consumer and prevent or slow down the decision process, but it can actually reduce satisfaction even when customers make the right decision. Less, as stated earlier, is often more in the consumer world.

There are numerous studies and publications centered on the "best" organizations, businesses, and agencies out there in business today. Bloomberg's *BusinessWeek* publishes an annual list of the "Service Winners," the 50 top-ranked service providers in industry. *Canadian Business*, *Forbes*, and *Fortune* all have their lists as well; we love to study the best companies and see what makes them tick.

Figure 2.2 is a summary of the available Service Winner rankings from *BusinessWeek* over a five-year period. What I have done with the data is to present the lists with only the companies who made *BusinessWeek*'s top 50 rankings at least three times in four years. Interestingly, 2012 was a special year for the rankings; while there were changes in the ranks of the various companies, no new companies penetrated my repeat winner list.

Now the list itself is interesting as it is, but the value, for our purposes, comes from examining the companies themselves. In almost every case, the repeat Service Winners on *BusinessWeek*'s list are companies we understand very well. There is nothing complicated about their service offering or who they are as an organization. One could argue (and I have) that Starbuck's menu board seems unreasonably complex, but once you have gone through the process a half-dozen times and been *trained* by the people around you in line, we tend to settle in. Otherwise, we go down the list and recognize quickly the value proposition of each firm very quickly—L.L.Bean is quality clothing sold primarily through the Internet; Lexus is about quality cars and quality service departments, as is Cadillac; Nordstrom is the upscale fashion retailer that combines great service with approachability.

None of the complexity discussed earlier is a surprise for most leaders and executives, yet it prevails. Why can't we be more like the Service Winners and keep it simple while delighting our customers? Those Service Winners will be the first to admit that they also suffer from complexity

2007	2008	2009	2010	2012*
1 - USAA	1 - USAA	1 - Amazon.com	1 - LL Bean	1 - USAA
2 - Four Seasons Hotels	2 - LL Bean	2 - USAA	2 - USAA	2 - LL Bean
3 - Cadillac	4 - Lexus	4 - Lexus	3 - Apple	4 - Lexus
4 - Nordstrom	6 - Starbucks	5 - Ritz-Carlton	4 - Four Seasons Hotels	6 - Starbucks
7 - Lexus	10 - Ace Hardware	6 - Publix Supermarkets	5 - Publix Supermarkets	10 - Ace Hardware
9 - Enterprise Rent-a-Car	12 - Ritz-Carlton	10 - Ace Hardware	6 - Nordstrom	12 - Ritz-Carlton
10 - Starbucks	13 - Amica Insurance	12 - Four Seasons Hotels	7 - Lexus	13 - Amica Insurance
11 - Ritz-Carlton	14 - Enterprise	13 - Nordstrom	8 - Ritz-Carlton	14 - Enterprise
12 - Amica Insurance	15 - Publix Supermarkets	14 - Cadillac	10 - Ace Hardware	15 - Publix Supermarkets
13 - Southwest Airlines	16 - Nordstrom	15 - Amica Insurance	11 - Amazon.com	16 - Nordstrom
18 - Apple	17 - Southwest Airlines	16 - Enterprise	13 - Starbucks	17 - Southwest Airlines
19 - Publix Supermarkets	20 - Cadillac	20 - Apple	14 - Amica Insurance	20 - Cadillac
22 - JW Marriott Hotels	21 - Apple	23 - True Value	18 - American Express	21 - Apple
	23 - Amazon.com	24 - LL Bean	19 - Enterprise	23 - Amazon
	24 - JW Marriott Hotels	25 - JW Marriott Hotels	22 - True Value	24 - JW Marriott Hotels
	25 - True Value		24 - Southwest Airlines	25 - True Value
13 firms	16 firms	15 firms	16 firms	16 firms

FIGURE 2.2

BusinessWeek's Service Winners, 2007–2012. (Data for 2011 is not available on BusinessWeek.com.) The number to the left of each firm is its actual top 50 ranking.

issues and related challenges. The larger question here is why this complexity prevails. Why are leadership teams not more focused on dealing with complexity?

The answer is as complex as the environment in some of these firms. Our survey data indicates that most executives are aware of the complexity; in fact, 70% of leaders believe they have too much complexity,[4] too much "stuff" going on in their organizations. These same leaders acknowledge that their customers do not value or understand half or more of their products or services. Think about that for a minute—executives are saying they have too much complexity in their organization, and that their customers do not appreciate or understand a large percentage of their product or service offering. This sounds like a significant opportunity, and something we will pursue further in Chapter 3.

In many cases, this acknowledgment of significant complexity is a hunch or feeling, an expectation that we should be performing at a higher level, but we are not clear why we struggle. I refer to this as organizational *scotoma*. A scotoma is a blind spot. Physiologically, they can occur in your eye, blocking vision and your ability to see out of certain parts of your eye. Far more common (and relevant to this discussion) are psychological scotoma. French philosopher Henri Bergson once said that "the mind sees only what it is prepared to comprehend." This means that your brain is making decisions about what it allows you to see or not see on a fairly

FIGURE 2.3
What do you see? (Originally from a nineteenth-century German postcard.)

regular basis, often as a result of a functional focus on one element of an operation while another is causing a larger issue.

Have a look at Figure 2.3. What do you see? This is a classic illusion, with the image of both a young women and an old woman embedded in the picture. Most people are quickly able to see both images, switching back and forth between them. Others (and this is not a test of intelligence, I assure groups when I run the activity as part of a complexity or Lean exercise) see one or the other, and struggle to see both. Their minds have decided which image they are able to see. In effect, the scotoma keeps them from seeing everything there is to see.

The same phenomenon happens within our organizations every day. People are so focused on the tasks and work before them they are unable to see the larger picture—the waste, complexity, process issues, and especially opportunities—which highlights the necessity for fresh eyes around the organization on a regular basis.*

Few dispute the presence of excess complexity in their operations. The question becomes, how do we deal with that complexity? In the coming chapters, we will discuss what I refer to as the agility cycle (Figure 2.4), an organizational enabler for the reduction of complexity throughout our corporate processes. The agility cycle relies on a clear understanding of our customer—who they are and what they want. That understanding then supports the role of Lean and a value focus, directing resources toward areas of benefit and away from areas of waste.

Metaphorically, we can say, then, that the customer is at the center of the agility cycle. The output of the cycle would be what we will refer to as an agile culture and an organization that chooses to compete on speed, simplicity, and a focus on customer wants and needs as the central strategy of the business.

As an agile culture is established through the organization as a result of these tools, advocates will also see a broader impact on the general behavior around the firm. Let's examine our practice of business meetings for a moment. In the United States alone, something like 11 million meetings are held each workday, costing corporations more than $37 billion per year.[5] Another study indicates we spend 300,000 person-hours preparing for and attending executive committee meetings.[6]

---

* Bring in a friend, mentor, or someone from another department or division. A past professor, uncle, or sister-in-law. Just bring them in.

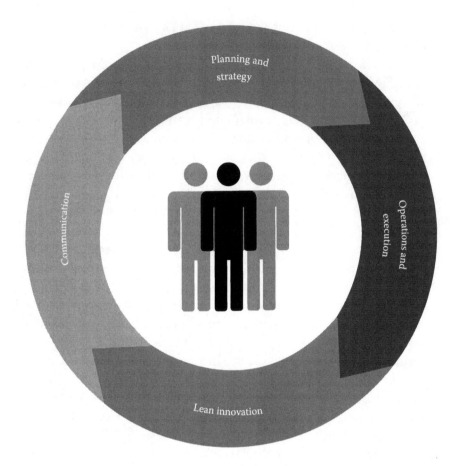

FIGURE 2.4
Agility cycle.

While the numbers themselves are staggering, a better indication of the impact of your meeting threshold may be a little self-reflection. Ask yourself these questions:

- How many meetings do you have scheduled weekly on your calendar?
- Can you rank those meetings in order of value to you, to the firm, or to the customer?
- Look at the bottom of the rankings for your meetings. When was the last time these lower-ranked meetings created any value? Is there any reason we can't eliminate or combine some of these meetings?

- Examine people's behavior in meetings. Are people arriving late, having not reviewed the agenda or prepared to contribute to or support the discussion? Are people too often in the Blackberry pose, hands huddled beneath the table typing away on their smartphone? These people are wasting not only their time, but yours.
- Are people within the organization practical about who they invite to meetings, or do they ask for everyone? Are agendas carefully created and distributed for every meeting? Are attendees and the chairperson diligent about sticking to the agenda?

Well-run, purposeful meetings are extremely beneficial for any organization. Innovation and problem solving are social processes, and any group gathered will be more effective than a single individual. A good meeting can communicate, remove obstacles, align interests and behavior, and work toward a common agenda. Even in a situation where the agenda is a bit looser, meetings can connect people and reaffirm relationships and team culture.

Agile organizations do not tolerate poorly run meetings or uncommitted attendees—people simply do not have time for waste or the abuse of their schedule, and they hold each other accountable. As we move forward through the book, we will examine how successful firms establish priorities and plans, and create alignment between their goals and operations. People in these organizations then understand how their work and role within the firm supports the "greater good" and how their area of responsibility is aligned to support strategy. In that state, they better understand the best use of their time, and jealously guard their schedules. This does not mean meetings are avoided, but participants and invitees will certainly insist on effective agendas, equal participation, and an alignment of the meeting subject to the firm's goals and objectives.

At the core of a firm with an agile culture is an appreciation of time. Meetings can solve problems and save us time, or they can consume resources and waste our time. The theme of this book—killing complexity in the interest of enabling an agile organization—centers on the idea of eliminating those barriers we discussed from Figure 2.1 and reducing complexity within the business. Loosely defined for our purposes, complexity is anything that keeps you and the team from focusing on value and what matters most to the firm—your customers. We can identify other effects of complexity as well, again generally related to time. More questions to ask are

- Do you, your direct reports, or managers receive texts or email related to work in the evening? Are employees expected to respond in the evening?*
- Do people take their phones and laptops or tablets on vacation?
- Are people tired? Does it appear that key employees are not getting enough sleep?
- Do people have time to occasionally goof off? That is, do they have access to periodic slack time to recharge their batteries, minds, and emotions?

When there are too many of the wrong answers to these questions (you do not need a rubric; you know the wrong and right answers), the organization is suffering from too much complexity. Periodic occasions of extreme scheduling, long days, and the resulting fatigue happen and are expected, especially when launching a project or solving a problem. It should never, however, be the norm. That peak resource consumption, if we can refer to it that way, should be held in reserve, ready to attack a challenge, new potential customer, or competitive threat. Keep the organizational engine running at 80%, and we will all feel lighter on our feet.

There is research to support these statements. A recent report indicated that firms with perpetually tired and overworked employees underperformed compared with those with well-rested employees, and actually cost those companies an extra $3000 per employee.[7] Overscheduling tasks, meetings, and events also limits executives to short-term linear thinking,[8] and pushes downtime off the schedule and into personal time. On the other hand, employees with access to periodic white space in their schedules are often quicker to come up with new ideas, products, and solutions, and generally challenge mediocrity. Most of us are familiar with people like Bill Gates or Jeff Bezos taking personal retreats; well, the goal of this personal time is to push the schedule back for a day or two, refresh and recharge while the day-to-day complexity is kept at bay.

So ask yourself, what would you do with one extra hour per week, if the clock fairy could grant it to you? For some, the answer would be sleep, based on the conversation above. For others, it would be time with their

---

* Sending email in the evening (or early in the morning) is not necessarily bad. That may be the time of the day that someone chooses to clean things up, or he or she may be working from a hotel or in another time zone (literally or figuratively). The negative aspect comes when the culture of the firm establishes a norm that email should be responded to when we receive it, regardless of the time of day.

family, or time with their development team or suppliers. Others would walk the floor or catch up with their customers. Whatever your answer (and this is key), write it down. Then, go out and find that hour. It is yours, so guard it jealously when you get it.

──────────

ONE LAST STORY

I want to compare a couple of products for you. This is by no means scientific, and may come off as peevish on one hand, and an endorsement on the other. I am okay with that.

I buy most of my dress shirts online. I have the retailer's sizing system figured out, they offer all-cotton shirts in a tailored cut, and it is a simple process to order. It does not really matter who the retailer is, because most retailers and haberdasheries* engage in a similar practice. The problem is how the firm packages the shirt, and most of you who wear the occasional dress shirt know what I mean. The packaging for a single shirt includes

- Clear plastic bag (this makes sense—keep the shirt clean)
- Boxboard form in back
- Tissue liner in back
- Boxboard collar stay
- Clear plastic rigid collar stay
- Clear plastic rigid top-button "holder"
- Rigid plastic sleeve clips

Thankfully, stick pins have been eliminated.

I appreciate that some of this is to keep the shirt clean, and in the proper shape. Cotton, especially, can take on a wrinkle or crease in perpetuity if hung, ironed, or packed incorrectly. At the end of the unpackaging process, however, I really feel like I have accomplished something, yet I have added no value to the shirt. My brother-in-law David reminded me that the same packaging strategy seems to apply to children's toys. So, here it is: *there has to be a better way.* Enough said.

───────────────

* That could be the biggest word in this book, and it certainly isn't *simple*.

Contrast this with a completely unrelated but very simple product: Apple's iPod Shuffle™. The Shuffle is now on its fourth or fifth generation (who cares, really), yet it retains its elegant design and simple operation. It is a tiny, square device with no screen, an on/off switch, and the standard Apple control wheel. Who is Apple's customer for the Shuffle? Generally, an athletic or active individual. The Shuffle will hold a couple hundred songs, has a spring clip for attachment to your shirt or waistband, and is rugged enough to withstand the bouncing and jarring of your exercise. Nothing more complicated is required for that customer's needs. While Apple's product development team is certainly not perfect, the Shuffle is dialed in, so I hope they do not change anything on coming generations of the device.

The evolving Internet of Things could go either way. Most of you are familiar with this product and service phenomenon. This is your connected world. The Nest™ thermostat gets a lot of the credit for kicking this off, but we can probably go back to your first Bluetooth™ device, where your phone connected to your car or drove music through a wireless speaker. Now, we can lock and unlock our home remotely, turn on lights around the house, manage a security system, or keep an eye on the kids. Most of this makes sense to me.

The challenge, then? Think back to your VCR days. (Ours, by the way, is still packed away in the basement for when our kids have kids and our then-grandchildren want to watch low-definition Disney videotapes at Grandma's house. We believe that will be a big deal someday. "Guess what Grandpa let us watch today!") Remember that flashing light on the VCR because the power had blipped and no one had reset the clock yet? Well, that was one device, and most of us ignored it. The Internet of Things relies on us establishing and keeping up the connections and settings now on multiple devices, apps, Wi-Fi, and software. Never mind that some kid in a smelly t-shirt jacked up on Mountain Dew can now hack my fridge; I don't think we will have the patience and diligence (vigilance?) to maintain the "system" and get the planned benefit from it. Developers will update the apps, Wi-Fi passwords will be reset, power outages will reset other devices, and we will have to reconnect. I do not know that I have it in me. And, it's damned expensive ($40 for a lightbulb, $250 for the lock on your front door, etc.).

While the millennials roll their eyes here, the rest of you are with me, right? More on this in Chapter 6 when we talk innovation.

REFERENCES

1. Egan, M. How Banana Republic is getting killed by fast fashion. *CNN Money*, November 10, 2015. www.money.cnn.com/2015/11/10/investing/banana-republic-gap-fast-fashion/.
2. Schachter, H. How Kraft turned less into more. *Globe and Mail*, November 12, 2014.
3. Schwartz, B. More isn't always better. *Harvard Business Review*, June 2006.
4. Survey of 140 executives and managers. Kingston, Ontario: Smith School of Business, 2010.
5. $37 billion per year in unnecessary meetings, what is your share? www.meetingking.com, October 21, 2013.
6. Maxed out meetings. *Canadian Business*, December 2014, p. 78.
7. Nelson, J. Dreaming of a good night's sleep. *Canadian Business*, May 14, 2012, p. 75.
8. Barmak, S. Why slacking off is great for business. *Canadian Business*, August 13, 2012, p. 60.

3

Simple Strategy and Building a Vision

If I had more time, I would have written a shorter letter.

Blaise Pascal*

How do you decide which restaurant to order a pizza from? This is perhaps one of the greatest dilemmas faced by diners everywhere on a regular basis. The problem? Most establishments market their product exactly the same way. "We only use the freshest ingredients!" "We use the best ingredients!" "Just like Mama used to make!" Well, I grew up eating Chef Boyardee pizza prepared out of a box, which was all we knew at that point, so that last example does not really appeal. The bottom line is that those taglines are all the same, meaning customers will not appreciate a meaningful difference between offerings.

Other establishments have abandoned those taglines altogether: "Large 4-item pizza $11.99! Add 4 drinks for $2!" Call now before this offer expires! These organizations are obviously competing on price, appealing to Stone's *economizing* customers from Chapter 1. In other cases still, technology has evolved to allegedly† simplify the ordering process, in that hungry customers can tap a few keys on an app from their favorite restaurant and the pizza shows up 45 minutes later.

---

* This was likely an approximation of Pascal's words, although it has also been attributed to Mark Twain, Winston Churchill, and others.
† I use the term *allegedly* here in a perhaps peevish expression of dissatisfaction with chain restaurants that no longer have local employees answering phones when you place an order, and whose websites are often very cumbersome to order from. More on this in later chapters.

I present this scenario to students on a regular basis as we get comfortable with the concept of knowing our customer. As you will appreciate, most students are on a budget, and are also very tech savvy. Students also work different hours than many of us. Pizza establishments located near campuses generally have a pretty good idea who their key customers are, and behave accordingly. They offer promotions and communicate those promotions effectively to students. They stay open late to capture studious academics and those just leaving the clubs. They sell by the slice for drop-in customers, and the head office had apps developed to enable their customers to order without using their phones the way they were initially intended (i.e., talking to someone). Students have pointed out that some chains now offer a tracking feature on their app, so customers know the exact status of their order.

None of these restaurants sell what any of us would call high-quality food, but they are for the most part successful on price and convenience. They understand their market and compete hard for each customer. The rub is that while most of us have a preference,* an idea of whose pizza is "best," most of these establishments are exactly the same. In fact, if our preferred chain went out of business tomorrow, we would move on, no hearts broken. This discussion, then, serves two purposes: First, it helps us appreciate the importance of knowing our customer and building our operations to serve those customers effectively. Second, it highlights the importance of differentiation within the firm's strategy. When we compete on price and convenience, and our competitors are equally economical and convenient, one of us does not need to be here.

Most business leaders and academics are familiar with the basic competitive options presented by Harvard professor Michael Porter in 1987, where firms can choose to compete through cost leadership, differentiation, or focus. While these concepts are no longer new or groundbreaking, they remain key strategic priorities for firms in most sectors of industry. That is, if our organization cannot find a way to compete through the provision of low prices or product or service differentiation, or develop expertise and focus, Porter's studies (and subsequent supporting research) indicate we are not long for this world. Our firm's

---

* For the record, I prefer local pizza operations over the chains when given the opportunity. Unique flavors, wood-fired brick ovens, and even talking to someone nearby on the phone all appeal to me.

strategy, then, needs to establish a path toward one of those three targets.*

What is strategy? Saying an initiative, product, or service is "strategic" is probably one of the most overused (and least understood) terms in business today. Some define *strategy* as how the firm makes money. While accurate, that definition is not specific enough for many purposes, and ignores many sectors, including not-for-profits, government, and education. Others describe it as pursuing particular businesses or sectors and, more importantly, how to compete in that sector. Dane Jensen, a colleague who heads up the strategy practice at Performance Coaching, simplifies this position a bit by saying strategy is a statement of where to play, and how to win.

These strategy statements are all accurate, and for many practitioners and executives, it really gets down to what language you are comfortable with. For me, that language circles back to my foundational questions: Who is your customer, and what do they want? If we can answer those questions related to your business, we can articulate a strategy. Strategy statements have other characteristics as well. A good strategy is simple, clear, and repeatable. People cannot do what they do not understand. The simpler and clearer that statement is, the better the team is able to understand the firm's strategy and, more importantly, appreciate their role in bringing that strategy to life. Good strategies also have to be actionable, relying on tangible, practical elements that teams can execute through the application of projects and other tactics. Strategy has short-term implications, brought to life in an operating strategy, and long-term outcomes achieved through innovation and a drive to get to what is *next* in our business, or the *big opportunity*. The key to an effective strategy statement, in my experience, is simplicity and clarity. The moment that strategy becomes too abstract, complicated, or unwieldy, the firm will struggle with execution.

There are as many approaches to expressing a strategy as there are strategies. The simplest and most straightforward method I have seen and

---

* In recent years, it has been argued that a fourth strategic option has emerged, that of *dominating* a sector and overwhelming the competition. Apple's iPhone, for example, offers neither focus nor low cost. It may be different to some extent as an operating system, but does essentially the same thing as Android devices. Its integration with other Apple devices, Apple's retail approach, and the massive app market, however, have created a huge following, making it hard for other products to keep up. Dominating strategies require platform-level capabilities, with supporting products, services, and systems that often enable the organization to shape a market, until the next platform-level innovation comes along to dominate the sector.

applied is what I call a strategy roadmap (Figure 3.1). The strategy road-map is a one-page expression of two key positions: first, who the firm is now and where they want to go, and second, who their customers are, and what those customers want. It illustrates the needs, gaps, and challenges the firm will face in achieving its vision, and also the tactics and projects necessary to resolve those gaps and deliver value for the customer.

The simplicity in this chart is by no means intended to be disrespectful of the strategy development process itself, nor the role an effective strategy plays in the success of an organization. Rather, it is the sum of the key

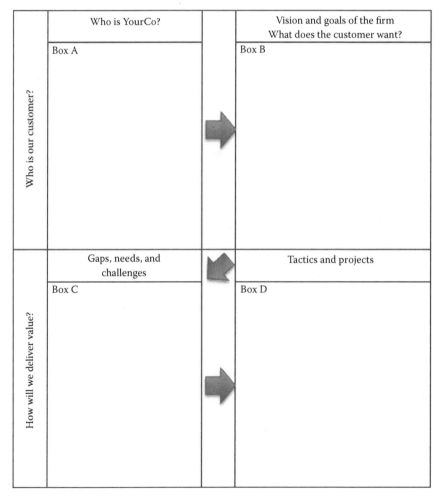

FIGURE 3.1
Strategy roadmap.

elements of that strategy expressed in a form that is, again, simple, clear, and repeatable.

BUILDING A STRATEGY ROADMAP

Let us examine the content of the strategy roadmap. Each of the main boxes in the framework (Boxes A–D) summarizes the different key elements of the organization's strategy and the *high-level* elements necessary to execute that strategy. This is just a single-page summary, so there really is not room for depth and detail; that depth comes later. For now, keep each box to five or six bullet points. Box A, for example, outlines the firm in its present structure: what business it is in, and who its primary customers are (e.g., number of locations, employees, and retail or fast food). It also gives a brief summary of the current state of the organization, good or bad (15 locations added in the last 12 months, sales growth of 12%). Box B is an expression of the firm's future state, or where it hopes to be if its strategy is executed effectively. Box B should include what we call a stretch objective for the firm, or our "big opportunity," as John Kotter calls it; if the goal was easily achievable, it is unlikely that the strategy provides any real differentiation for the firm, and mediocrity continues. Box C, then, highlights the gaps, needs, and challenges associated with achieving the firm's vision, or the difference between where they are now (Box A) and where they are going (Box B). Do not underestimate the importance of Box C; if Box B expresses true differentiation for the firm, there will be skills, resources, or other challenges faced in executing that vision. Box C is a summary of those challenges. Finally, Box D expresses the key projects and tactics necessary to close the gaps in Box C and bring the vision of Box B to life.

Another perspective on the roadmap is illustrated in Figure 3.2, what I refer to as the strategy roadmap order of process. That is, the top half of the roadmap is an expression of who the firm is now, and where it is going, while the bottom half is how the firm plans to get there, or execute that vision. You will also notice the arrows highlighting the direction of thought process within the strategy roadmap, lighting the path from Box A, to Boxes B and C, and then to Box D in the shape of the letter Z. Through application with both leadership teams and groups of students, the strategy roadmap quickly earned the nickname Z-chart, appropriately acknowledging the flow of work in building the chart.

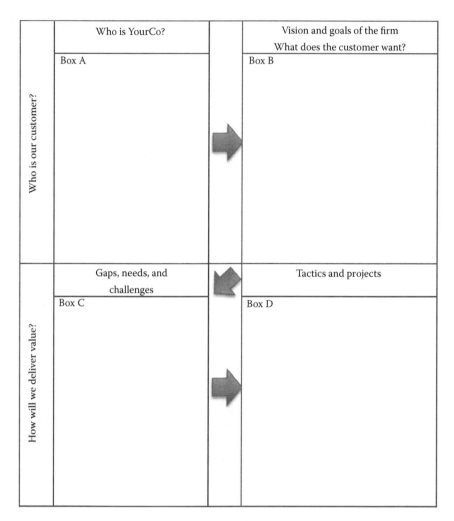

FIGURE 3.2
Strategy roadmap order of process.

We can also divide the chart by who does the work. The top half, or strategy portion, is generally the turf of the organization's executive leadership, or even its corporate offices if such a thing exists within the firm. This group is responsible for building a vision and enabling the coalition of remaining resources to execute. The lower half of the chart, or execution portion, becomes the realm of business unit managers or tactical managers. This breakdown of work will be familiar to many of you with experience in strategy development, where the executive body decides what business we will be in, the business unit managers then determine how to compete in that business, and an operating strategy is developed to support that overall corporate strategy.

The goal is to keep the Z-chart to one page, with each box having roughly half a dozen key points. Together, this chart of four boxes is a summary of the strategy and direction of the firm. Some organizations I have worked with have "prettied" the chart up with their logo, enlarged it, and posted it in key places around the organization in recognition of the framework's true purpose of being a simple, clear, and repeatable expression of organizational strategy. Keep in mind that distilling down a firm's direction like this into a single page will not be easy (with a nod to Lean theory and the old quote that saying something is simple does not mean it will be easy). Forcing that simple summary, however, keeps leadership on point, and prevents it from drifting in focus from the needs of the target customer.

The benefits of simplifying our customer and strategy message in this fashion are significant. Think of the power and clarity for your sales team when there is a common understanding within the firm of who the primary customer is. The sales team then knows they are not isolated or acting without the support or resources of the organization. Everyone, including engineering, operations, and sales, is now pulling their oars in the same direction.*

Clarity is important to the investor community as well. In one global study, European analysts rated "clear, well-communicated strategy" as very high in importance to issuing "buy" recommendations on companies within their sphere of influence.[1] It is hard to say if this element of consideration should be increasing or decreasing in importance as more publicly traded firms evolve with no clear indication of how they make money. The onus seems to be on the investors, in many cases, to figure this out for themselves.

I have developed a Z-chart for a fast-food chain in Figure 3.3, Fast Burgers and Sandwiches (FB&S).[†] Box A illustrates the type of business that FB&S competes in, the number of locations, and who its customers are. Box B then expresses the future direction of the firm as it looks to streamline its operations and increase customer satisfaction in their target segment. Box C summarizes the gaps and challenges it faces, and Box D outlines the key steps and tactics it believes are necessary to execute its strategy.

---

* For more on this, see also "Dismantling the Sales Machine" by Adamson, Dixon, and Toman in the November 2013 issue of *Harvard Business Review*.

† Any similarity between FB&S and other franchises or chains is entirely coincidental, but quite possibly very familiar to readers. Perhaps an incident of déjà vu.

Who is *Fast Burgers and Sandwiches*?		Vision and goals of *FB&S* — What does the customer want?
• FB&S is a fast-food chain, with 1200 franchises across North America • Customers are economizing and convenience buyers • The menu includes ~60 items, including a variety of burgers, fries, chicken and fish sandwiches and wraps, sodas and shakes • 75% of customers order from 25% of the menu • Quality is average and comparable for this segment • Employee turnover is slightly higher than average for this segment		• Increase product and service quality to rank in the top 3 in our segment within three years • Reduce employee turnover by 25%, and earn a reputation as a fun place to work in a part-time and casual employment • Leverage these points to attract new franchisees and add 300 locations within five years • Create a brand that emphasizes that fast food does not mean sacrificing quality or service (big opportunity)
Gaps, needs and challenges		Tactics and projects
• Too many menu offerings for newly hired cooks to prepare consistently • Employee turnover leads to training gaps with part-time staff • Menu size creates bad decision risk for customers and slows ordering process • Menu size also dilutes marketing and supply chain efforts • Head office spends significant time on human resources and menu-related work		• Reduce menu by 50%; focus on items ordered most often by customers • Reallocate corporate resources to improve hiring and training practices for franchisees • Improve relationship with suppliers; focus larger percentage of annual buy with few suppliers to improve quality of inputs • Invest in kitchen technology where appropriate to simplify and automate preparation process • Concentrate marketing theme on quality and experience at FB&S

Row labels (left margin): *Who is our customer?* (top), *How will we deliver value?* (bottom)

FIGURE 3.3
Strategy roadmap for FB&S.

We will briefly examine the content and implications of each of the boxes in FB&S's Z-chart. Who is FB&S (Box A)? Here, we describe the current state of its business, including locations, the type of business it is, and any demographic and behavioral information we may have. As noted earlier, we want the good and the bad; it is important to be brutally honest in this box about the current state of the business, especially areas of competitive weakness or customer dissatisfaction. These elements become opportunities for improvement.

The vision and goals of FB&S described in Box B represent the desired future state of the business. These notes may include growth or development plans, technology enhancement, or improvements in customer satisfaction, but must improve on any weaknesses expressed in the first box. Goals and objectives should be as tangible, specific, and measurable as possible. Our big opportunity here is to reshape our customers' perception of what fast food can be.

Box C summarizes the primary obstacles FB&S will face in moving from its current situation in Box A to the future state in Box B. In this case, the reader will note a relationship between a menu with too many offerings, impact on kitchen operations, staff training and experience, and customer satisfaction. That is, if Boxes A and B outline what the customer wants, what do we need to do to bring that to life? What are we missing? The final box on the Z-chart then outlines at a macrolevel the projects that resolve the gaps and challenges of the previous box, or begin to create the future state of the business outlined in Box B. While the points in Box D give us a sense of what the firm plans, the reader will appreciate that this level of detail is appropriate for discussion and communication, but is really not sufficient to be actionable.

This is an important point. The strategy roadmap by itself provides a number of benefits to the organization—it simplifies our strategy and summarizes the key elements of that strategy for the organization; it highlights the challenges the team will face, and then outlines some of the key next steps for the firm. By itself, however, the roadmap is not actionable; while many leadership teams will stop at this level, there is insufficient detail here to enable the organization to deliver on its agenda. We will resolve this deficiency with the introduction of two other tools, the customer value map and the operating plan, in Chapters 4 and 5, respectively.

For some organizations, the future state of the business is very specific, resolving current operational or customer challenges, like at FB&S. Ultimately, if we are honest about FB&S, its future depends on it being able to solve these issues; fast food is too competitive an industry to endure with mediocre strategy and execution. If we were to ask the executives at FB&S our question—*If FB&S ceased to exist tomorrow, would anyone notice?*—its honest answer should be no.

Other organizations seem to endure for generations, migrating successfully from one direction and existence to another. They appreciate where they have come from, but they do not cling to it, building on their experience and history as they pursue new paths and directions. These are companies like 3M, IBM, Johnson & Johnson, and even less tenured firms like Virgin. For executive teams in these firms, the statements for the future state of the organization often feel a bit more open-ended. These businesses consider mega trends within business and society, recognizing that solving higher-level challenges not only provides greater net benefit, but also will create new niches in business they may be best positioned to capitalize on. Society-level challenges today are many, but could include concerns such as air quality, water availability, food safety, and accessible health care. Consider water alone on that list, and we quickly see opportunities with systems and technologies that may provide access to safe drinking water in rural and remote parts of the world, or the pursuit of desalinization technology in places like drought-ridden California and Israel. In these firms, such higher-level challenges lead to innovation agendas creating larger societal value. Long-term corporate survival is never fully assured with such a perspective, but it is certainly more fun than scrapping for survival every quarter. A bullet in Box B for one of these firms might look like this: *high-quality products and services that satisfy verified customer needs.**

As an aside, some of you will have noticed we are not taking the traditional path to strategy with the evaluation or creation of a vision, mission, or values for an organization. Many advocates will argue that leadership should always start with vision, mission, and values, as that will crystallize why the firm exists, and what its purpose really is. I generally disagree. The application of vision, mission, and values statements describes how we want the firm to think, and there is a big difference between the thinking and the doing. While these statements absolutely have a place in all our organizations, I will continue with my themes in this book of keeping it simple, and advocating for our customers. Therefore, rather than pursuing statements of how the firm *thinks*, we will continue to develop tools that describe how we want the firm to *work*. We will also focus our operating strategy on the true purpose of the organization, and that is the creation of value for our customer.

---

* A 3M objective, as stated by Managing Director, UK (retired), Jim McSheffrey.

Many companies and executives talk about the importance of their customers; fewer walk the walk. Boston Consulting recently noted that when asked, the customer is by far the most often cited priority in their business. Further investigation of these organizations, however, indicated that less than half of their business decisions considered customer insights, and only a third of firms actually built the customers' perspective into strategic planning, capital investment, and other operational decisions.[2] More and more, we are operating in isolation, either failing to consider our customer and market, or waiting for something significant to happen in that market to spur the firm to action.

At the time of writing this book, and for the previous number of years, Western society was mired in what I refer to as the *Sleeping Beauty economy*. It seems that since the financial crisis nearly a decade ago, executives, boards, governments, and policy makers have been waiting for something to happen. There are obviously exceptions, with some stimulus spending or energetic leadership teams committed to the creation of value. For others, however, the "time is not right," and I hear this time and again. While we wait for the prince to appear, we seem to have forgotten that economic growth relies on the appropriate application of land, labor, and capital. I appreciate that this view is somewhat simplistic, and those resources are limited (more on that in Chapter 4), but it really is up to each and every one of us to find a way to drive the organization forward on an ongoing basis.

Sometimes, that means taking on work that others deem less attractive. I spent a number of years while in industry with a manufacturer called Autosystems, a private automotive parts company that worked with a number of car companies, from General Motors to Aston Martin. We were approached numerous times through the 1990s by customers or competitors looking to outsource a piece of work that was too small of a job (i.e., insufficient volume), too complex, involved a challenging process, or was honestly just something their union did not want to do. We took on 90% of this work, usually at very good margins, and almost always with some good-natured resistance from our engineering and manufacturing people. We would hear comments like "Ford couldn't figure this out, and you want us to?" or "Why do we want to take their crap jobs?"

Some of this work was absolutely "crap." Volumes were predicted to be low already, and then fell off the map entirely after a year. Tooling provided by a customer produced poor-quality parts that we had to deal with. Parts for assemblies were designed by customers, in some cases, that had no means of joining or attaching related components, resulting in significant mechanical engineering and design work on our part to get the system to work. In every case, however, the team found a way to make the project work, and ultimately we delivered value for the customer and our organization. Skill sets were developed that did not exist previously at Autosystems, new customers were acquired, and very often, it was some of this crap work that filled in the valleys of a very cyclical business. Tackle the job, solve the problem, and do the work now. When we wait, we lose. When we stand still, the market passes us by.

The Canadian currency has swung significantly versus the U.S. dollar, British pound, and euro over the years, and there are pros and cons to both a strong and weak currency. When the Canadian dollar is weak compared with the currency of its peers, exporters enjoy lower costs as their labor is paid in a softer currency. The trade-off is that many investments made by Canadian firms are more expensive, as technology, equipment, and other capital are often sourced from the United States and other countries. When the dollar is stronger compared with the U.S. dollar, investment becomes more affordable, but execs complain their business has dropped off due to the relative strength of the currency and insist they cannot afford to invest in productivity-enhancing equipment. So, we sit and wait, and Sleeping Beauty slumbers on while some firms rely on the exchange rate to compete.

A Deloitte study on the Canada–U.S. productivity gap[3] highlights some of the numbers. As labor costs in Canada rose with a strengthening Canadian dollar between 2000 and 2007, per worker investments in productivity in Canada were only 52% of the corresponding U.S. investment, *this when those investments would be more affordable due to a stronger Canadian dollar*. Productivity growth in Canada over that period was only 25% of the productivity growth in the United States.

While the message here is simple and clear, the implications for leaders are far from easy. Emerging from the Sleeping Beauty economy requires a less risk-averse perspective, and acknowledgment that executives own their own destiny. We cannot continue to rely on the North American Free Trade Agreement (NAFTA) and other free trade agreements to be competitive.* All the more reason to focus on developing market-centric

---

* Especially when we lag behind most countries in the extent of our free trade agreements. Chile, for example, had 52 such agreements as of 2013, while Canada had only 10.

strategies that enable the firm to deliver value to today's customers while thinking about tomorrow's.

Delivering the most value also takes more than getting off our tails and working at it. Numerous studies refer to a lack of effectiveness of strategic planning altogether, often indicating that perhaps 1 in 10 plans are executed effectively, with firms delivering half of the performance committed to in their plans.[4] If we believe that people cannot do what they do not understand, it stands to reason that the strategic plans themselves need to be simple, clear, and repeatable, with a core focus on delivering value. Simplicity itself, though, is an elusive target.

Apple, for many years, embodied the idea of *simple*. Apple computers "booted" up more quickly; iPods and iPhones synched simply with music and video files on your home computer; buying and sorting music was a dream; software upgrades were not forced on users, but sat quietly in the corner waiting for the operator to download. Today, some elements of Apple's extended empire have grown unnecessarily complex, with engineers and designers seemingly taking the position of "What else can we add?" rather than "What does the customer really need?"

iPhones now have factory-installed apps that cannot be removed, several of which are unwanted for many of us (e.g., the Health, Podcasts, and Apple Watch apps). At best, additional features clutter the screens on your devices, while at their worst, they drain the battery in the background, or potentially enable others to track the user's whereabouts or location. Many postings on user forums express device owners' frustration with Apple for assuming they know best what users want and need on their products, futilely looking for advice on how to remove the apps altogether.* Complexity rarely leads to improved customer enthusiasm.

In some ways, the emergence of complexity inside Apple may be merely a result of its growth. The firm has a market capitalization of a half-trillion dollars, with cash on hand comfortably in the billions. With that size and reach, creative minds can have a natural tendency to develop and implement ideas faster than they kill the old products and services in the firm. I believe it is more often due to the natural inclination toward entropy and disorder in the systems and operations that make up an organization. Think about your garage, for example, and how quickly

---

* I maintain a love–hate relationship with Apple—there are many aspects of its designs that drive me crazy (short drive), such as mandatory apps like Find Friends that cannot be deleted. I still remain a fan of the company itself and its products at the macrolevel.

it gets cluttered and jammed after you spend a Saturday cleaning it up. The same phenomenon applies around our workplace, product design, or service portfolio—without engaged leaders actively forcing the team to link processes, features, and services back to customer needs and the organization's strategy, extraneous elements settle in and become embedded like that stack of boxes in the garage. Pushing back on organizational entropy takes work and a continual sense of the firm's strategy and purpose.

The spirit of Steve Jobs remains, however, as Apple continues to resist unwieldy productization,* holding with just three primary models of iPhone and four models of iPad at the time of writing. Any variation in products tends to be related to processor speed or storage. Also, they tend to take the lead on the removal of features from product designs as new technology emerges. MacBooks have been sold without optical drives (CD and DVD) for several years, and Jobs drove the elimination of cooling fans in MacBook Air almost 10 years ago. Several competitors in the smartphone market, on the other hand, became known for their model proliferation, complicating supply chains and project launches and confusing sales staff and customers.

General Motors has long been known for its brand and product proliferation, yet for years seemed oblivious to the impact on both the organization itself and its customers. Even after the sale or elimination of several GM brands following bankruptcy in 2009, the organization still seems to struggle. Most of us know that a side-by-side comparison of the Chevrolet and GMC pickup trucks would produce few real differences, yet GM continues to design, tool, validate, manufacture, and sell both brands, at redundant costs of tens of millions of dollars and thousands of man-hours every year. Advocates within GM still believe they have customers that will only buy a Chevy or a GMC, and believe they will lose customers if they killed one of the brands. I remain skeptical.

In February 2016, Toyota killed its Scion brand. After years of investment in a brand targeted at millennials and first-time Toyota buyers, sales remained below expectations. Resources are being directed toward other opportunities within the larger Toyota organization. A number of other

---

* *Productization*, in this sense, is the proliferation of products offered by the firm. (Cross, B., Paquette, J., Service Complexity and the Perils of Productization, *Ivey Business Journal*, January/ February, 2014.)

firms exhibit simple, easy-to-understand strategies and execute accordingly. As examples,

> FedEx competes on speed.
> Southwest and WestJet Airlines deliver good service at relatively lower prices.
> Disney is about entertainment and family experiences.
> Zara and Forever 21 compete with expedited forward fashion.
> Wal-Mart is low cost.
> Menchie's is designed on consumer customization and control.
> Amazon is about convenience.

How clear is your operating strategy to customers? Do people understand your key offering and the way your business works? Can customers really tell you apart from competitors? Big banks, telecoms, some restaurants, and retailers like Home Depot and Lowes struggle with this last point, ultimately relying on location or price as key competitive elements.

Firms like FedEx are easy to understand, and FedEx has remained so since its founding 45 years ago. After pioneering the idea of overnight shipment, FedEx remains focused on the idea of moving our goods and information from point A to point B more effectively. Innovations and enhancements are based on customer value, such as the implementation of ground service for less urgent packages and real-time visibility on our shipment's location with the advent of the Internet, GPS tracking, and other technologies. As customers, we understand FedEx and the value it provides.

Here are some questions for consideration as you examine your strategy with the goals of simplicity and clarity, not only for your customers, but also for employees and members of your extended enterprise:

- Do customers understand the real value your firm provides?
- Is your strategy simple, clear, and repeatable for the team responsible for its implementation?
- Are there instances of unnecessary product or service proliferation in your portfolio? Can you eliminate products or services without causing undo stress to operations or the customer?
- As you reallocate resources within the firm, can you enhance service performance above levels considered normal within your industry?*

---

* I refer to this as *servitization II*, and will discuss it further later in the book.

> Seattle's Virginia Mason Medical Center benchmarked Toyota in Japan in the reduction and elimination of waiting rooms and procedure delays. Now patients show up at their appointment time and walk right in.

- Are we spending more time on our mission, vision, and value (how we think) than on our strategy and operating plan (how we work)?
- When thinking about the firm's direction, do we compare ourselves to the competition, or evaluate customer behavior and needs, looking for gaps and opportunities? Lexus, for example, did not benchmark Cadillac or Lincoln, but watched how customers used vehicles, moved stuff, and went about their lives. For their service centers, they spent time with Four Seasons rather than competitor service departments.[5]
- Do we look outside our industry or field for solutions to our problems? Chances are that we are not the first to face this issue, and someone else has already solved the problem in some form.

Pursuing a simple strategy is certainly not a simple exercise, and my approach is by no means intended to diminish its importance to the organization. For me, it really comes down to the perspective that people cannot do what they do not understand; if the team cannot connect their roles and responsibilities to your strategy, their ability to execute that strategy will be severely diminished. Apply the single-page model outlined in the Z-chart; if you can get the strategy and direction of the firm to that one page, the rest of our activity throughout the book will be so much easier to implement. For one thing, the primary role of leadership after the construction of that Z-chart is to support the team and respective business units in the execution of that strategy, and that is where the fun happens.

━━━━━━━━━━

ONE LAST (CONTINUING) STORY

Over roughly a decade at the helm of General Motors, Rick Wagoner and the leadership at GM continually underperformed both the industry and stock markets. During his tenure, GM lost more than $85 billion, $70 billion of which was lost during the last four years of his role as CEO.[6] Many say that GM lost money because it built cars people did not want to buy. Others (myself included) believe GM consumed too many resources trying to keep up an unreasonably diverse portfolio, and therefore failed to do anything at a level better than its peers (including product design, engineering, and service). Throughout that period, and culminating in its bankruptcy in June 2009, GM failed in a number of ways, but our focus here is on its failure in the eyes of its customers. During that period,

- GM cancelled its leading-edge electric vehicle (EV) program and made no significant investments in hybrid vehicle technology.
- The company launched several major recalls of a million vehicles, each for issues like faulty wiper motors that failed in the rain or tailgates that broke when sat on. Defective ignition switches allegedly leading to accidents and deaths were designed and built into millions of vehicles over this period as well.
- GM allowed its number of brands to grow to 13, several of which have since been shut down or sold. In many cases, brands within the GM portfolio operated dealerships across the road from each other.
- GM's administration drove the organization into such poor condition that GM churned through three CEOs in five years following its Chapter 11 bankruptcy, before appointing the capable (by most early accounts) Mary Barra in 2014.

Throughout this period, there was a serious lack of accountability at the senior levels of GM. Even during the final four years of his tenure, when GM lost that $70 billion, Wagoner removed virtually no senior executives from their post. Even if there were no direct lines between these executives and the failures of GM (doubtful, perhaps?), we have to ask ourselves on an ongoing basis, "Would I hire this person again, knowing what I know now?" Sometimes the answer is no, and we need to move on.

While Rick Wagoner was at the helm of General Motors for 10 years, and without doubt bears significant responsibility for its performance over that period, this situation is far larger than one man. The decline of GM was in a bigger way a result of the structure of the organization, and a lack of a clear customer-driven strategy. GM was simply too complex an organization to plan, communicate, and execute effectively, something I witnessed firsthand over a 15-year career in the automotive industry. Twin platforms like Chevy and GMC pickup trucks or the

Chevy Cavalier and Pontiac Sunfire required twice the tooling, investment, and expensive engineering labor to develop and build, and twice the number of dealers to sell. Complicated process reviews and redundant meetings were a hallmark of their development process (I will acknowledge unconditionally that GM staff and engineers knew how to run an effective meeting—they certainly had enough experience with it). Various divisional headquarters were located in numerous locations around Detroit, Michigan, and in fact the United States, making communication and face-to-face meetings more challenging.

From a strategic perspective, redundancy and "more" seemed to be the mindset for the firm, rather than "better" in any way, with no real consideration of a clear target customer. Everything about GM's complex operating strategy noted above was built with the goal of trying to appeal to all customers in the automotive market, a strategy we all know is unsustainable over the long term. A firm cannot be all things to all people, and the structure, brand, and product proliferation at General Motors was trying to do just that. It had three brands of luxury cars (Cadillac, Buick, and Oldsmobile), three brands in the United States alone for middle-market buyers (Chevrolet, Pontiac, and Saturn), two truck brands, and even a military-style SUV brand in Hummer. Porter's competitive strategy options (low cost, focus, and differentiation) did not include a "most" or "biggest" category, and surely GM did not achieve a *dominance* position. If we want to win, we need to know our customer, and then be the best at delivering value to that customer.

Up to the bitter end, GM executives fought for the retention of all their key brands—they firmly believed that there were customers out there who would only buy a Pontiac. As a condition of the $30+ billion bailout package in 2009, however, the Obama administration required that GM

Pre-chapter 11		Post-chapter 11
13	**Brands**	8
5900	**Dealerships**	5000
91,000	**Employees**	68,500
47	**U.S. manufacturing plants**	34

FIGURE 3.4
General Motors then and now.

eliminate or sell a number of its brands and simplify both its product line and organization. The deal also required Wagoner to resign. A comparison of the old GM versus the post–Chapter 11 GM looks like Figure 3.4.

The organization is still far from agile, but it has improved. I am skeptical, however, that current leadership appreciates the benefit of reduced operating complexity on the business and suspect that the "clean garage" will quickly begin to fill with clutter once more.

I need to say in closing that I got to know many first-class people at GM and its subsidiaries at the engineering, purchasing, and operating levels over the years, people who were honestly as frustrated with the organization from inside as we were from the outside.

REFERENCES

1. Groysberg, B., Healy, P., Nohria, N., and Serafeim, G. What makes analysts say 'buy'?" *Harvard Business Review*, November 2012.
2. Barton, C. The introverted corporation. BCG Perspectives, April 27, 2016.
3. The future of productivity. Deloitte, 2012. https://www2.deloitte.com/ca/en/pages /insights-and-issues/articles/future-of-productivity-2012.html
4. Cespedes, F. Putting sales at the center of strategy. *Harvard Business Review*, October 2014, p. 24.
5. Taylor, W. *Practically Radical*. New York: William Morrow Press, 2011, p. 69.
6. Simons, R. *Seven Strategy Questions: A Simple Approach to Better Execution*. Watertown, MA: HBR Press, 2010, p. 84.

4

Lean and Enabling Agility

There is nothing quite so useless as doing with great efficiency something that should not be done in the first place.

Peter Drucker

Adding buttons isn't Innovation. Removing them is.

Recent advertisement for Acura

<Command-Q> A simple command to exit a program on an Apple MacBook

<Alt-J> A pretty cool alternative music group

Almost a decade ago, Passport Canada faced a dual-pronged challenge— increase the security of the passport and documentation process for Canadians, yet reduce the time and complexity associated with applying for or renewing a passport. At the time, there were something like 30 steps associated with issuing a passport in Canada, many of which were simple checks or approvals by different parties in the process. An application could sit for days in the queue awaiting a task that really added no value to the process to be completed, but the step had been part of the process for years. The result was that the process of issuing a passport typically took six weeks, with associated costs increasing all the time. Many of these steps were added for a reason over the years, solving a problem in some way, but the system evolved and today's challenges are different, making much of that existing system unnecessarily complicated.

At the same time, pressures from both within Canada and the international community to increase the level of security of the application process, the identification system, and the issued passport itself increased.

Stephane Cousineau* headed up the project on behalf of Passport Canada. You can appreciate that driving change is never easy, and inertia can be especially substantial within government. His team succeeded, however, in both enhancing the security of the documentation process, with numerous images and features in the passport, and reducing the renewal process by up to five weeks. Steps were eliminated, and other steps were automated. Applicants now enter their data directly into Passport Canada's information system, where they are prevented from moving from one field to the next until the field is filled out correctly, eliminating mistakes that slowed down the previous application process. The documents are now better and more secure, and customers often get the new passport within a week of applying.

In 2008, Maple Leaf Foods in Canada kicked off a Lean campaign in the interest of refreshing their product portfolio, overhauling manufacturing processes and enabling agility. At the time, Maple Leaf had 78 different flavors of hot dogs and wieners in its line, and as many as 50 different sizes of dogs. How many flavors of hot dog do you really need? While those numbers are incredible by themselves, the larger impact was on the shop floor, where changing the line from one flavor or size to another was extremely cumbersome, often taking up to 90 minutes to complete.

By 2015, Maple Leaf had completed most of the turnaround,[1] closing nine facilities with low productivity, investing in state-of-the-art processing technology in a new Hamilton, Ontario, facility, and eliminating redundant product lines, including dozens of flavors and sizes of hot dogs.

Tim Hortons, purveyor of coffee and donuts in the hypercompetitive fast-food industry since the 1970s, began expanding its product line a couple decades ago to include soups, sandwiches, and other lunch and dinner fare to expand beyond just breakfast and capture more traffic throughout the day. As it expanded, however, it found service slowing, lineups lengthening, and customers becoming dissatisfied. Tim's has done a pretty good job over the years of removing a product from the menu as it has added others, yet increasing traffic for lunch and dinner meant higher demand for a more diverse menu than it had witnessed in the past.

---

* Stephane is a friend and MBA alumnus of Queen's University. He is kind enough to return to speak in our classes on a regular basis. Stephane was the CIO of Passport Canada, and has gone on to take senior roles at Elections Canada, the Department of Foreign Affairs, and other key portfolios.

In February 2014, the firm initiated a significant streamlining of processes and menu items, including killing a number of long-term products, such as specific muffins, cookies, and even popular donuts like the honey cruller.[2] Menus were made simpler to read and food processes were simplified, making room for both improved customer service and potential new menu items in the future.*

In December 2014, the Ontario government passed the Better Business Climate Act that would enable the reduction of red tape for businesses and reduce unnecessary regulatory burdens by $100 million by the end of 2017. At the start of 2015, the provincial government claimed it had reduced regulatory requirements by 17%, looking to speed up and streamline business regulations and strengthen key clusters deemed important to the province. This is a great step, and an example that Lean applies to government as well, yet there is a long way to go. It still takes four to six weeks to issue a new provincial driver's license or health card after the applicant has provided all necessary information, provided a photo, and paid any relevant fees.†

When we hear stories like these, examples of organizations across numerous industries finding a way to reduce complexity and increase their agility, we wonder why the improvements are not more widespread. In fact, the more we know about good service and good performance, the less tolerant we become of inefficiency and poor service. Examples of inefficiency (like the issuance of a new driver's license above), complexity, and poor automation implementation abound.

- Airlines allow you to print boarding passes at home (or store them on your mobile device), yet force you to line up at the airport for a similar check-in process to drop any checked bags.
- Prescriptions, including prepackaged dosages, often take 30 or more minutes to fill.
- Automated kiosks for payment and checkout at retail locations and check-in at airports often do not work or require an agent's assistance.
- Time-consuming updates or upgrades to computer software or applications.

---

* Donut update: Tim Hortons has since realized its catastrophic mistake and brought back the cruller.
† How interesting would it be if the federal government and provincial or state governments shared information, and especially their successes, to a greater level. The feds solved the application and renewal process 10 years ago, and the province of Ontario is still struggling with 6-week renewals.

Sadly, we are all too familiar with examples such as these where processes or service has broken down, resulting in poor outcomes for both the organization and its customers. Worse, most organizations fail to recognize that this gap between the intent of their service and the outcome of the process exists. Bain & Company call this a "delivery gap," and published a startling study related to that gap. In its study of almost 400 firms, 80% of those firms believed they provided superior service to their customers. When the customers of the same firms were queried, only 8% believed they received superior service from those firms.[3] I do not think any of us are surprised by the fact that this delivery gap exists, but the magnitude of the difference of opinion between the firms and their customers is certainly significant.

There are a number of reasons this situation exists. Leadership in many cases underestimates the effort it takes to build truly good customer relationships, resulting in customers who may be satisfied but not enamored. In most cases, organizations struggle to both identify who their best customers really are and design an experience or product to suit that customer. I introduced this discussion earlier in the book, and in this chapter, we apply a tool called a value map to help refine our understanding of those customers. What I have found in many situations is an organization trying too hard to please customers with a broad selection of product or service choices, or not paying enough attention to the customer-facing processes supporting those products and services.

We will explore the paradox of customer choice for a moment, where in fact numerous studies have shown us that there is a fine line between not enough choice and too much choice. The impact on both our operations and customer enthusiasm is significant. In one study, researchers offered consumers a choice of two DVD players; 32% said they would buy model A, while 34% said they would buy model B (interestingly, 34% were undecided). When offered only one model, however, only 10% of consumers indicated they would buy that machine.[4]

In Chapter 2, we discussed another piece of research, where a social psychologist set up a tasting table inside a store, and every few hours she would switch between offering 24 flavors of jam and offering only 6 choices. Fewer options for customers led to a greater conversion rate from curiosity to actual sales. This study is from the mid-1990s, and perhaps familiar to some of you already, but its implications to leadership are significant. Consumers need some choice, but too much choice leads to problems.* Anxiety and bad decision risk increase. How many times have you regretted your meal choice when you see what arrives for your dining partner? Even when we are happy with the outcome, the time to make decisions increases with more choice, resulting in queues and the consumption of operating capacity.

In the mid-twentieth century, Princeton professor George Miller studied our capacity for options and found that most of us can only cope with between five and nine pieces of information at any time,† after which our rational decision processes begin to bog down and emotion rears its ugly head. Some firms have taken steps to ease the decision burden on consumers and make their own operations more efficient at the same time. Costco offers far fewer choices than most retailers, including only four types of toothpaste (vs., say, Wal-Mart, which may carry up to 60 sizes and types of toothpaste). When Proctor & Gamble reduced the number of varieties of Head & Shoulders shampoo from 26 to 15—eliminating the poorest sellers—sales increased 10%, production planning was simplified, and inventory costs went down.

More often than not, however, choice, complexity, poorly designed services, and processes continue. Most leaders acknowledge this complexity. Why do we not fix these situations, then? More common than we would like to admit, the real challenge is actually being able to see where the problem lies within our firm. We know we have a problem, but we fail to see specifically where it is. I call these situations organizational scotoma or process blind spots, as introduced in Chapter 2. Our job in this chapter is to understand simple tactics that will enable the organization to see through those blind sports and focus more clearly on areas of customer value.

I will break these tactics into three categories: mental calisthenics, customer visibility, and process visibility. I should state clearly at this point that this chapter is not a "how to" guide to implementing Lean. For any organization that has taken that significant step and started its Lean journey, suggesting you could implement Lean with a few tools from a single chapter in a book would be disrespectful of the effort and dedication it truly takes. While I have assisted a number of organizations with Lean, my intent here is to help people not only recognize the complexity within

---

* And obvious operational problems for the firm itself as complexity increases.
† Perhaps supporting our fascination with the number 7. Seven numbers in a phone number, seven habits, seven deadly sins, seven colors in the rainbow, and so forth. With a nod to Stephen Covey, one wonders if there are more than seven habits of highly effective people, but since we can't handle more than seven, the truth would make us *less* effective.

their business, but also begin to deal with it. As I indicated in Chapter 1, there is literally a ton of Lean material out there already, whereas our focus here is more on the idea of reducing complexity in the interest of increasing organizational agility.

We will start with *mental calisthenics*. Many groups I work with want to jump right to a particular problem or process where they are experiencing difficulty, which is perfectly natural. There is often some urgency associated with the problem, with related customer issues or internal dissatisfaction. Tackling the problem head on, however, can lead to resistance with the team responsible for the process, or slow progress as a result of the scotoma discussed earlier—the team is too close to the problem.

Most facilitators and consultants have a few favorite exercises or activities that are intended to pull people back a bit from their day-to-day work and help them look at their problems from a higher level. Two of my own exercises are the Lean alphabet and the paper airplane exercise. I will generally run both, and the total time spent on the exercises, including debrief, is about 20 minutes—perfect as ice breakers and to get the group thinking in the right direction.

The Lean alphabet goes like this: Indicate to the team that *Oxford Dictionary* has contacted you and is in the planning stages for the next edition of its online dictionary. But, in a move to differentiate the Oxford product, their personnel are looking for ways to eliminate some of the redundancy of the English language (i.e., words with different meanings, same-sounding words, etc.). They plan to start the exercise by eliminating several letters from the alphabet. Their goal is to be able to make all the same sounds, but they believe they can accomplish this goal with as few as 20 letters, over the existing 26. From there, tell the team the task is on them and have at it.

The exercise takes about five minutes, and as you write the letters down on the board, also indicate how they suggest making a particular sound if that letter is eliminated. For example, if we eliminate *J*, the soft *G* can be used to make the *J* sound. Here is a summary:

Eliminate	Replace With
J	Soft G
F	Ph
C	K, S
Q	K
X	Eks, S

As you wrap it up, write a sentence on the board that illustrates what the impact of that Lean alphabet might be. For instance,

Gak be nimble, Gak be Kwik, Gak Gumped over the Kandle Stik

or

We are Kustomer Phokused!

Lesson: Even something as seemingly fundamental and rigid as the alphabet could be *improved*. Is it likely society would do this? Doubtful—check with me when the United States adopts the metric system—but one may note that much of our approach to texting relies on using abbreviations and fewer letters in the interest of expediency.

The paper airplane exercise is done in groups. Break the team into groups of four to six people, and give them five pieces of paper each. I sometimes use a template, with the folds necessary to build the desired model of aircraft indicated on the paper. Hold up a finished model of the plane in your hand, and indicate this is a competition. The teams are competing against one another for bragging rights (or a trophy, if you really want to get serious about it). Each team needs a timer and a quality inspector. The timer records the total amount of time to build and test the five aircraft, while the quality inspector inspects each craft to ensure it looks correct, and then executes a test flight (my rule of thumb is the planes have to fly 10 feet). Ask the group if they have any questions, get the stopwatches (smartphones) ready, and go!

You can add some music while people are folding away. If you have access to the Internet, the theme song from Jeopardy™ is good for a laugh. As teams finish their five aircraft, write their times on the board or easel, and then have them return to their seats.

In discussing the exercise, first, look at the variety in completion times on the board between the teams. For me, having run this exercise north of 100 times, the average times are around 3–4 minutes, with the best time across all events being 56 seconds, while a number of teams earned the mercy rule, approaching 8 or 9 minutes with no end in sight. Connect that variation in time back to any task in the organization. Different people, different times, and different results equate to variability, which is waste. What would it take to get everyone working at the same pace?

Second, pick up a few of the aircraft and compare them with your model. You will see a number that are very different than what the "customer" was looking for. This variability in outcome can be attributed to experience, training, and even the quality of instruction, both within the exercise and back at the workplace. Tie that back to the quality of instruction the last time they dropped an assignment off to one of their direct reports. "This is what I need. How is two o'clock for you?" And then we walk away before we ensure they fully understand the task, often leading to some variability in outcome and anxiety on the part of the employee doing the work.

Third, ask what the team observed among themselves while they tackled the activity. A few teams will delay the folding until they have talked about how to divide the work—well done! Communicate, agree on objectives, divide the work by skills or expertise, and proceed. These teams typically come in at between two and three minutes. Most teams, however, jump right into the construction of the planes, with results ending up all over the place.

Finally, ask them if they could improve their time if you were to provide more templates and they repeated the exercise. Most nod their heads, eager for a second crack at the exercise. It was fun, after all. Hold up one of the planes, now, as this is the key learning. *More important than doing a process faster*, you say, *is determining whether we should be doing it at all.* Look again at Drucker's quote at the start of the chapter. What we are really looking for is a reflection on the value of building this aircraft in the first place. Rather than doing it faster, should we be doing it at all? How much value does this paper airplane really create? Will our customer pay for this plane? How many more of these aircraft are there around the organization?

This is the essence of Lean for me and for the organizations I work with. Sure, we can improve the process of how we build and test the planes— this is process visualization, and the next step in this chapter. Of far more value for us as an organization, however, is identifying and eliminating the processes around the firm that add about as much value as building the paper airplane. Then, think about what you would do with the time if we could eliminate that process.

Both of these activities are fun—you will see smiles very quickly, even among some of the more uptight or senior members of the group. By nature, in fact, the people earning six- and seven-figure salaries in the room are as competitive as anyone. The exercises themselves are intended to highlight a couple of very simple concepts, while at the same time pull people back from their day-to-day experience. Spending 20 minutes relaxing the group and breaking the ice while introducing critical Lean principles is never a waste of time. From there, we can talk process visualization.

PROCESS VISUALIZATION

My premise here is we cannot fix what we cannot see. The activities above are the first step in alleviating some of our organizational scotoma, but there is nothing quite so effective as mapping it out on paper, or other media, as we will see in a moment. Figure 4.1 illustrates a process we are all familiar with, arriving at an airport through to boarding an aircraft.* While there are numerous different figures or symbols possible in process flow analysis, the three that are most relevant for me in the majority of situations are the task (a box or rectangle), buffer or queue (or delay in the process, indicated by an inverted triangle), and decision (indicated by a diamond with one line in and two out). Arrows to the next figure connect the symbols.

We could argue that there are other steps associated with this process that have been omitted, such as having our checked bags weighed, tagged, and placed on the conveyor, or a gate agent inspecting our photo identification before we board the aircraft, but this diagram is intended to illustrate the process rather than be comprehensive.

Professional tools (including Microsoft Office programs) exist that facilitate the construction of high-quality process flow diagrams. This is terrific if you need to present the material to an executive or a client and have someone within the firm who can polish the model once it is mapped out. For most of us, however, I advocate keeping it simple. Get the team together (after running exercises like the Lean alphabet and paper airplanes) and draw the challenging process in question on the whiteboard. This can take an hour or more, especially with a complicated process (I had a government client indicate to me that it took them over a year to map out one such complicated, interdepartmental process, but once they mapped it, improved it, and rolled it out, it proved to be extremely robust), so ensure you have blocked out sufficient time to complete at least the initial mapping. Then, test it. Do we have all the steps? Are they in the right order? Avoid trying to fix or eliminate anything before the process is complete.

---

* I have intentionally left out the drive to the airport, traffic, and parking to reduce the stress associated with reading this section.

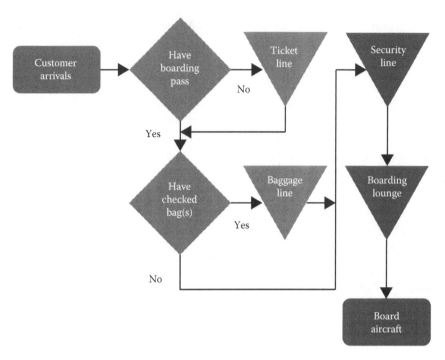

FIGURE 4.1
Airport check-in process.

Some guidelines in the initial process flow mapping are

- Bigger is better. Make the diagram as large as you can accommodate. If that means using a full 4 × 8 whiteboard, so be it. You want it to be visible and clear for the full group, and large enough to photograph with your phone if you have to adjourn before completing the exercise.
- Fewer words are better. Each task, buffer, or decision box is not an opportunity for a paragraph. Keep it to as few words as possible for clarity on the chart.
- Some groups prefer to use large Post-it notes as each task box, and then stick the Post-it notes on easel paper. In this case, use Sharpie markers rather than pens or pencils. The process flow diagram is now portable should you need to use it for demonstration purposes or to return to the meeting at a later time. Post-it notes also enable the team to move tasks around on the board during the analysis and review process.

- Some of your processes have an impact on physical operating capacity, and therefore involve a time component. As you measure and evaluate these processes, indicate the time each step takes in or under the task box.

Mapping the process is the tedious part, but it is essential in setting the table for the team to drive true value and start eliminating the "paper airplanes." A note on language here: I refer to this work as "process visualization" or "process mapping." You will have heard of value stream mapping, or creating process flow diagrams. It is all basically the same thing, where the "value" in value stream mapping comes from inserting the perspective of the customer and what they want and need in your analysis. I think we are doing that regardless.

Once the process has been mapped, have a quick discussion about the history of the existing process. Why is it done this way? Often, the process was developed or adapted to solve a problem. Does that problem still exist? You may hear that this is the way "we have always done it." If the initial creators of the process are still in the organization, it is obviously helpful if they participate in the process. As you evaluate the process, here are some things to think about:

- Count the steps and evaluate how much time it takes to get through the whole process. How many different people, desks, or operators are involved?
- Look for breaks or delays inherent in the process. How long does it take for that step or work to be approved? Is that approval still necessary?
- Look for travel time for parts, work, or documentation between steps. Is that time or distance necessary? What would happen if the two tasks were side by side?
- Can a task be completed by the customer as part of the application process, or can work be outsourced to third parties? You do this now when you buy an airline ticket online, select your seat, and print off your own boarding pass at home.*

---

* An interesting side note: Customer satisfaction increases as you give more control to your customer. In this case, getting the customers to do some of our work for us makes us more efficient and, in fact, increases customer satisfaction at the same time. This is pretty much a win–win.

- Where are the constraints or bottlenecks in the process? How do we alleviate them? This may be with additional resources, technology, or ideally, reducing the work associated with that task.
- Do operators with decision responsibility have everything they need (information, empowerment, and tools) to make immediate decisions? Does that executive or manager really need to approve the work at that stage, if at all?
- Use a facilitator—someone familiar with Lean, process flow diagrams, and visualization tactics—who can keep the process moving and help the team get through their first Lean activities.

Question each step or task in the process. Ask why we do it that way, how often does something "bad" happen with this step, or when the last time was that we failed to receive approval at that step. Small victories are fine the first few times a process is reviewed in the organization. Look for both the low-hanging fruit and easy fixes, along with one or two more challenging processes. I like to target at least one process review per month as the firm gets its legs under it, but keep in mind the improved process may not be perfect yet. Tweak it, tune it, and follow up as necessary to ensure the team continues its focus on customer value. Would the customer be willing to pay for that?* If the answer is yes, make it better. If the answer is no, kill it. Either way, celebrate the victories and stay involved with the process visualization as leaders and managers.

CUSTOMER VALUE MAP

This is a good place to circle back and discuss the customer. Developing effective processes, eliminating waste, and focusing on what we call "value" requires a clear understanding of our customers, and my core questions: Who is our customer? What does that customer want?

Value maps have been around in a number of forms for years, often called perceived value diagrams or attribute maps. They are good comparative tools for evaluating where competitors stand against each other when analyzed versus a number of industry comparables, such as cost,

---

* A favorite quote of my friend Darren Dalgleish, CEO and general manager of St. Lawrence Parks Commission in Ontario, Canada.

service, or location. Figure 4.2, for example, compares Company A versus Company B on a number of elements in the consumer electronics industry.

As we analyze Figure 4.2, we can see quite quickly how Company B may provide superior product features and benefits, but (as we would expect) the firm charges more for those product advantages. We can also see that Company A provides improved customer service, and perhaps launches more effectively (possibly as a result of the relative simplicity of its product).

This type of competitive analysis is common, whether it is on behalf of Company A, Company B, or perhaps a third-party analysis of an industry. The charts and analysis associated with competitive analysis take many forms, but when conducted objectively, we quickly get a sense of how the firms stack up.

Analysis like this, where we review our firm against the competition, is important, and most organizations are well served to maintain a current picture of their industry standing. Too many firms, however, stop there,

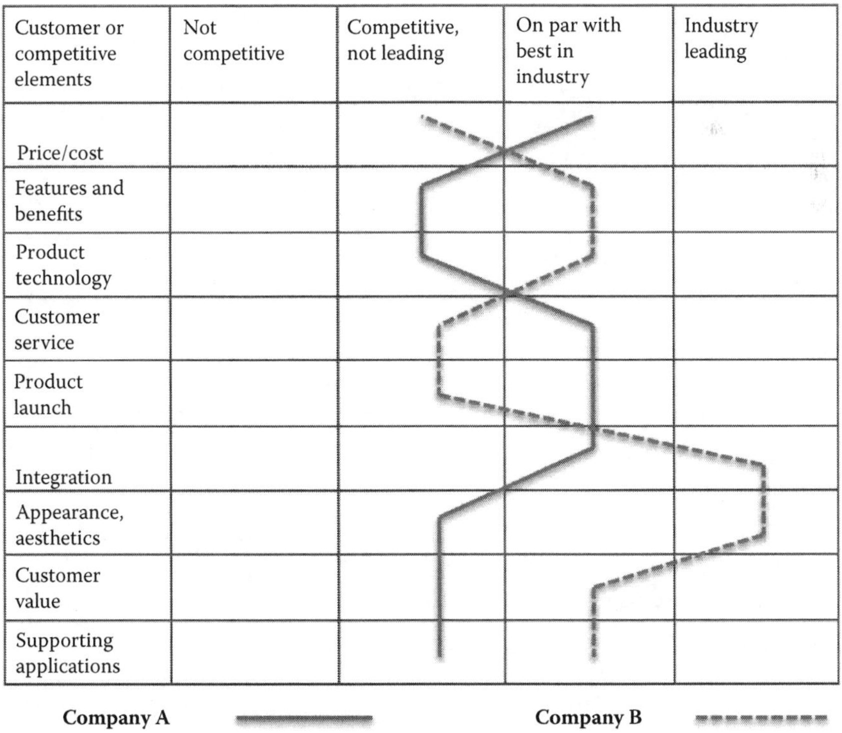

Customer or competitive elements	Not competitive	Competitive, not leading	On par with best in industry	Industry leading
Price/cost				
Features and benefits				
Product technology				
Customer service				
Product launch				
Integration				
Appearance, aesthetics				
Customer value				
Supporting applications				

Company A ⬛⬛⬛⬛⬛⬛ **Company B** ▪▪▪▪▪▪▪▪

FIGURE 4.2
Customer value map for two firms in consumer electronics.

under the traditional perspective that the competitive landscape is their sole yardstick. There are several problems with this viewpoint: Firms that strive to match competitors based on this analysis cannot excel in the customer's mind—they all feel the same. Also, there is little real attention paid in this analysis to what the customer really wants, which means we may be overspending in some areas and underspending in others, and not know it. When it comes to the allocation of scarce resources in any organization, this is a key challenge. Finally, the tool as is does little for organizations where the idea of a "competitor" is less defined. Think government agencies, not-for-profits and charities, education, or health care.

With all this in mind, I like to take this value analysis to another level, and compare our organization against the desires or needs of the customer. In Figure 4.3 (OurCo vs. the Customer), Company A becomes OurCo, and the other line represents our target customer. I have shaded and highlighted the "gaps" between OurCo and its customer for ease of discussion.

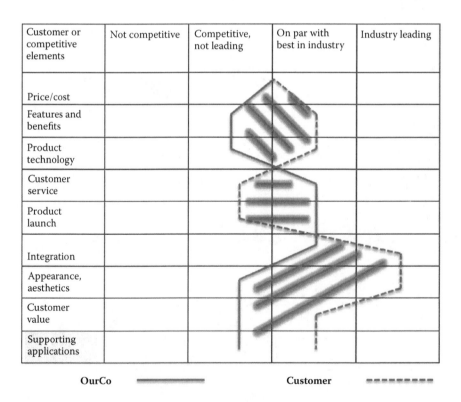

Customer or competitive elements	Not competitive	Competitive, not leading	On par with best in industry	Industry leading
Price/cost				
Features and benefits				
Product technology				
Customer service				
Product launch				
Integration				
Appearance, aesthetics				
Customer value				
Supporting applications				

OurCo ▬▬▬▬ Customer ▬ ▬ ▬ ▬ ▬ ▬

FIGURE 4.3
Customer value map for OurCo vs. customer expectations.

This perspective provides significant value. Gap A, for example, suggests that the customer may not be as price sensitive as we currently believe, and that they are willing to pay for increased product performance, features, and benefits. At the same time, they rely less on customer service and care less about how well we launch new products. Appearance, integration with other technology (e.g., the Internet of Things), and value are more important to the customer as well.

Take this discussion to the strategy level. If (big if) we want to increase our investment in technology and features with respect to our product and close Gaps A and C, where will the resources come from? This work could be R&D, engineering, additional supply chain capability, and related investment in new or augmented product and performance capability. This gets back to our Lean discussion from earlier—scale down in areas that customers are less interested in, and move those resources to new or more important areas within the firm. In this case, we could dial down investment in customer service (Gap B) and free up that investment to spend on technology.

In this manner, the customer value map is intended to be used in conjunction with the strategy roadmap, presented initially in Chapter 3. In that chapter, we discussed the gaps, needs, and challenges associated with the firm's strategy and enabling the future state of the organization. Content for Box C in that framework (illustrated as Figure 4.4), then, can be augmented with the gaps developed in the customer value map. The two frameworks are, as a result, developed concurrently, where Boxes A and B of the roadmap are built first, followed by the value map, enabling Boxes C and D in the roadmap to be completed. As we proceed to subsequent chapters in the book, these two foundational pieces of organizational planning will support the creation of the organization's operating plan, which is where the team's real work is detailed.

A necessary point at this stage in the discussion is the element of trade-offs. An effective strategy for the organization not only outlines what we will do, but also appreciates what we will not do. As we all realize, no organization succeeds in the long term trying to be all things to all customers. If we pursue fast and agile, for example, comprehensive product or service platforms would bog the execution of that strategy down. This trade-off is reasonably clear to most of us in in our strategy and planning.

Less clear, however, is the trade-off associated with the day-to-day activity and work around the firm. The question from earlier: If you had one more hour per week, what would you do with that time? The problem, it

Who is *OurCo*?		Vision and goals of *OurCo* What does the customer want?
Who is our customer? • Designer, manufacturer, and retailer of consumer electronics, primarily in mobile phones • Supply 10%–15% of the market as of 2016, depending on country • 6000 employees in 8 countries • Considered a low-cost product that "does the job" • Strong corporate sales historically; declining consumer sales		• Survival in the short term (three years) • Develop key skills internally or with third party supply partner enabling product technology superiority • Build off product capability growth to strengthen brand • Establish stand alone online retail channel
Gaps, needs, and challenges		Tactics and projects
How will we deliver value? • Customers looking for features and benefits beyond current product capabilities • Appearance considered plain, average • Devices need to connect and support a broader range of other household devices • Engineering and technical skills currently inadequate to meet these demands • Customer service (a core competency in the past) is deemed less important to today's customers		• Recruit, train, and develop necessary technical resources for next-generation product family • Investigate contract design houses and supply partners able to support technology vision • Develop customer service strategy that more closely aligns with customer need • Market study to determine customer behavior trends as foundation for technology development

FIGURE 4.4
OurCo strategy roadmap.

seems, is even larger than freeing up an hour or two. More and more organizations are increasing their spending on employee wellness programs, primarily as a result of fatigue, stress, and the resulting loss in productivity. The bottom line: Our employees feel pulled in numerous directions, perhaps in support of an unrefined strategy or lack of clear objectives. We are wearing our people out.[5] The impact of that phenomenon is reduced productivity, lower morale, mistakes, and health issues. As an example, in a three-month study of only 18 hospitals and clinics, Dr. Kim Sears found 372 medication errors or near misses as a result of workload, distractions, and communication issues.[6] Whatever other resource challenges we have, time is often now the scarcest.[7]

Let's assume your employees are productive when given the opportunity, and then consider what the organization does, permits, or builds into policy that creates a barrier on that productivity. Burdens on our time are many, but as an example, we will evaluate briefly our behavior within corporate communication and meetings. Long email chains and "Reply all," regularly scheduled meetings and repetitive conference calls should all be subject to the "value test"—if the customer would not pay for it, find a way to eliminate it. We tend to treat other scarce resources with far more diligence than we do our available time.

Do a quick self-examination:

- Estimate how much time it takes you to review and properly deal with an email. Even if we were very optimistic and said one minute, next look at how many emails you receive per day. Many managers and executives now are averaging between 100 and 200 per day, or an average of roughly two hours per day of email.
- See if you can go an hour without checking or looking at your phone. Tech analyst Mary Meeker reports that many users consult their phone 150 times per day.[8]
- Audit a few emails sent to a group and look at the people cc'd. Do all those people really need to be part of this conversation?
- Count how many emails you receive related to a particular meeting, including postmeeting follow-up.
- Make a note on a Post-it next to your desk or work area for a day and track the number of interruptions to your work. If you can, time how long you can go, on average, working without interruption, including self-induced interruptions when you respond to the computer indicating you have new mail.

Very quickly, we get a sense of how little of our time is actually our own. Gregory Caimi discusses why this happens in his research related to time as a resource in our work lives, including managers gaming meeting calendars (accepting invitations to conflicting meetings and deciding later which to attend), a lack of controls (few accounting systems put costs on people's indirect time), and the presence of few consequences for the ultimately unintentional abuse of time within most organizations.

If we accept that a primary responsibility for an executive is to direct the attention of his or her team toward work and activity that matter, then we should further accept that in some cases, enabling the abuse of time as a resource within the firm is disregarding that responsibility.[9] Focusing on the customer as work that matters is one perspective. Another perspective considers the time the firm spends exploiting current opportunities and its strategy, and also the time spent exploring new opportunities. How well are we, in fact, focusing our resources on that exploiting and exploring? We will look at this again in our discussion of innovation later in the book.

Earlier in this chapter, we looked at process visualization, enabling the improvement of processes and focusing more resources on value creation. *Time* is more abstract, so perhaps we do not spend enough time thinking about *time*. Ultimately, though, consider the simple argument that consuming less time on a task equates to spending less money. Fast = less cost. Does that not sound appealing? Agility, therefore, is cheaper. Freeing up one resource (time) results in savings of another. What would you do with that hour saved every week? Write down the answer, and then find a way to take back that hour.

Employees like Wally from *Dilbert*™ aside, we have to work under the assumption that most of our team does not intentionally goof off. We believe the same about ourselves. Unintentional abuse of time, then, is a factor of numerous conditions around the organization, such as a lack of alignment, poor assignment handoffs, onboarding and training, failure to communicate priorities effectively, or a lack of engaged leadership. Lean is a focus on value, and therefore what matters most to our customers and the firm. When we understand and appreciate who our customers are, and what makes them tick, aligning our resources and even our own time becomes far simpler.

ONE LAST STORY

At one point in my career, I spent a lot of time working in Mexico. The company had purchased the operations of Wagner Lighting, and we were consolidating their operations into both our existing facilities in Canada and a plant Wagner owned in Matamoros, Mexico. The people there were a mix of locals (Matamorians?), employees who had moved to the Maquila* region from other parts of Mexico, and Americans who crossed the border twice a day to and from work at the facility. Regardless of where they came from, the entire group were terrific people and extremely welcoming to any of us, especially when we were the outsiders who had purchased their company and were now effectively sticking our noses in their business. It was common to be invited to dinner at a restaurant, or even their homes.

One middle manager, whom I will refer to as Carlos, asked one day if I would like to buy some authentic Mexican blankets to take home to my family. I had brought souvenirs home from Mexico, Brazil, China, and Europe in the past, so I agreed enthusiastically (although my wife has never been a fan of my Ming vase from China, apparently made in Hau "Charlie" Ming's factory in Shenzhen). Carlos said we would head over to his aunt's place after work and I could look some of the blankets over. She and her family made the blankets by hand themselves up in the hills, where it stayed much cooler through the day, I was told.

A bit more background here: Our plant was about 10 minutes from the border, and the route into the plant from the border stays pretty much to the developed commercial and hospitality areas of Matamoros, which are quite safe. Get off the beaten track, however, and you need to be careful, like in many parts in the country. The city itself is large, and after a number of years of Maquila-fueled growth, its population is approaching half a million people. We headed out later that day, with Carlos driving. After 15 minutes, we were getting into the less developed areas of Matamoros. The further we went, then, the more appreciative I became that I was with Carlos. Still, another 10 minutes later and I was getting a bit nervous.

Eventually, we stopped and he parked his car. We were now in a part of the city the tour guides and police officers tell people like me never to visit. I thought Carlos was secretly smiling to himself as we walked the two blocks to his aunt's place, as I was huddling closer to him than I would otherwise. People leaning in doorways and against cars and trucks on the street paid attention, nudged each other and pointed at me. I realized I should have called home before this sojourn and indicated my plans, and perhaps my location. I am sure you are sweating just reading this.

---

* Maquilas, or maquiladoras, are regions within Mexico where firms may import materials or machinery duty- and tariff-free, and then process those goods and export them. Aggregate costs on the manufactured goods are consequently lower.

Carlos's aunt's place was a basement flat, down a half flight of stairs. Dark, poorly lit steps. Getting down the steps required us to move between four large men who were wearing sombreros and ponchos and holding rifles, with toothpicks or cigarillos in their mouths under massive moustaches. One of them, whom I believed I recognized from a movie, might have been carrying a machete.

Carlos knocked on his aunt's door and walked in. I followed quickly. He called out to his aunt, and she came out of a back room. She was an octogenarian, weathered, somewhat stooped, with piercing dark eyes. Carlos introduced me, and she came over and took my hand in both of hers, turning it over and examining it for several seconds. I held still, hoping I would not be given bad news. "This line here? It says you will die today, Señor Cruz."* After a while, she nodded, released my hands, and beckoned us into the main room, where rack upon rack of blankets of all shapes and forms rested.

The blankets themselves were very nice, thick, and soft in a myriad colors. After the drive, and Carlos's not inconsiderable time and hospitality in bringing me there in the first place, I was not going to leave with just one blanket. I ended up with several, each selection earning a nod of approval from his aunt.

Now, most of you know that a tenant of any purchase in Latin America is the negotiation process. The haggle, the back and forth. "Señor, how can you? I must feed my blind, legless children!" Not this time. Carlos's aunt indicated the prices were about $30 per blanket, and I paid, lest the machete-wielding caballero at the top of the stairs be summoned. Thirty dollars each is very fair! Thank you! Carlos, let's go! Quickly, before the sun goes down, and we did. Somehow, we made it back to the car, and back to the plant, where I headed for my hotel.

By this time, I felt pretty good about my purchases. I had *authentic* Mexican blankets! The days of mocking my Ming vase were over. The anxiety of the process itself added to the value already inherent in these quality blankets. When I returned home, I told the story of buying the blankets again and again. Friends and family were amazed at both my bravery and the quality of work of the Mexican craftsmen in the hills outside Matamoros. I gave a couple of the blankets away to people especially close to me, and kept one that we still have up at our cottage.

---

* Carlos and a few of the others, in fun, convert my last name on occasion to its Spanish version.

The blankets had true value to me as a customer because of their authenticity. The acquisition process only enhanced the value—the adventure in acquiring them, the interaction with Carlos's aunt, and the craftsmanship of the hardworking people in their village up the hills were all part of aligning a product and service to the needs of a customer. Value was established several times over, that is, until we visited my sister-in-law's cottage a few years later, where on their couch was one of the *exact same* blankets.

"How did you get that?" I asked. "Were you in Matamoros? How did you meet Carlos?"

"Who is Carlos?" she answered. "We bought that from a guy on the beach in Cancun! Pretty cool, eh? Twenty bucks!"

REFERENCES

1. Atkins, E. Maple Leaf Foods finding success after 7-year organizational overhaul. *Globe and Mail*, April 30, 2015.
2. Atkins, E. Cruller fate: Tim Hortons cuts menu as it tackles long lineups. *Globe and Mail*, February 21, 2014.
3. Allen, J., Reichheld, F.F., Hamilton, B., and Markey, R. Closing the delivery gap. Boston: Bain & Company, 2005.
4. Mochon, D. The value of choice. *Harvard Business Review*, October 2013, p. 30.
5. Colvin, G. The new trend? Reducing stress in the workplace—By order of management. *Fortune*, July 24, 2014, p. 42.
6. Sears, K. Queen's led study sheds light on medication errors. *Queen's University Alumni Review*, Issue 2, 2014, p. 12.
7. Caimi, G. Your scarcest resource. *Harvard Business Review*, May 2014, pp. 74–80.
8. Scott, A. Giant slayer. *Canadian Business*, September 2014, p. 10.
9. Goleman, D. The focused leader. *Harvard Business Review*, December 2013.

5

Execution and the Operating Plan

Your customers are buying your execution, and not much else.

Barry Cross

"What can *we* do?"

Sadly, this question is all too common among the variety of organizations I work with, and perhaps is a familiar question to many of you as well. The root of the question relates to the ability of employees at their level in the organization, or employees within their particular industry. What can we really do at our level? How can we make progress where <insert excuse here>?

I will certainly not deny that barriers to change exist. We have talked about them throughout the book from multiple perspectives, angles, and directions. People who see themselves as having been denied enough times begin to doubt whether any progress is possible. The *culture of "no"* and the *legacy of failure* become their reality. This was especially prominent within several government organizations I worked with, particularly at the middle-management level. While they acknowledged that change was necessary, they really believed there was little they could actually do until management changed.

To some extent, this is true. Without the endorsement, direction, and leadership of the top levels of their firm, little long-term sustainable progress is possible. At the individual level, regardless of position and rank within the organization, however, there is still potential. Culture is central to the theme of this book, and we will investigate both individual and systematic approaches to creating an agile culture in this and coming chapters.

Let's examine a scenario, a situation that will be familiar for many of us, regardless of which side of the discussion you are on. An executive of Company A, who we will call Elizabeth, stops at the desk of a team member named Kevin and asks for a marketing communiqué to be prepared. Kevin naturally asks when Elizabeth would like it done. Elizabeth replies, "As soon as possible." Now, the employee in question is busy already, and has a number of other tasks in the queue. This new assignment will take at least a couple hours to complete properly. How the situation evolves from here, and the impact of the request, depends on the organization.

In Company A, Kevin sees this as another in a long line of last-minute requests from Elizabeth and other executives within the firm. Everything is urgent, top priority, and ASAP. Many of the requests do not even feel like they are part of Kevin's responsibility, but he is not really sure and has not had time to clarify this in the past. Kevin has no real sense of how his role supports or impacts the direction of the organization, but assumes that to some extent, people like Elizabeth have both his and the organization's best interests in mind. Employees are tired and morale is low as a result of long days and the accumulated backlog of work, and no end appears to be in sight.

Over at Company B, leadership spends a great deal of time communicating "the plan" to employees, and puts a priority on ensuring people understand how their role supports the vision and direction of the firm. Employees are expected to ask questions and get clarification when things are unclear. Urgent and last-minute work still happens, but when it is aligned to the strategy of the firm, it is far easier to get behind that task as an employee. In this case, Elizabeth's request is related to a new initiative the firm has been discussing for some time, but is finally ready to kick off. Kevin is familiar with the initiative, and commits to getting it done that afternoon.

In both firms, the work will get done. In the second firm, however, the request is less likely to be viewed as a result of Elizabeth's inability to manage her own schedule, and more likely a result of organizational readiness to proceed with the new strategy. Some people, unfortunately, are always running behind schedule, and the situation with Company A tends to individualize the larger organizational circumstances, even if Elizabeth happens to be managing this time well. Kevin's question that led the chapter, "What can I do?" highlights the position that he is rather stuck with things as they are. At Company B, the request is one piece of a larger puzzle that everyone understands, where both Elizabeth and Kevin are just filling their roles.

We will circle back to communication and culture in Chapters 7 and 8, respectively. Our immediate priority here and now is to build on the strategy discussion from Chapter 3, and enable the organization to develop and present clear priorities across the broader organization. Figure 5.1, the A^3 ("A three") change realization model, represents the outcome of the models and frameworks discussed in this book, the strategy roadmap, the value map, and in this chapter, the operating plan. The A^3 represents the state of being, if you will, of an agile, execution-minded organization. The A^3 itself is not actionable, but is the result of the application of these other tools. In those organizations where we apply this system, we see resources *aligned* to the purpose and direction of the firm, we witness employees and team members who understand and *appreciate* how their roles support that organizational direction, and we communicate and follow-up, *assuring* the completion of those roles and responsibilities.

Toward the end of Chapter 4, we were examining the impact of wasted time. We can extend that discussion with the belief that the continuance

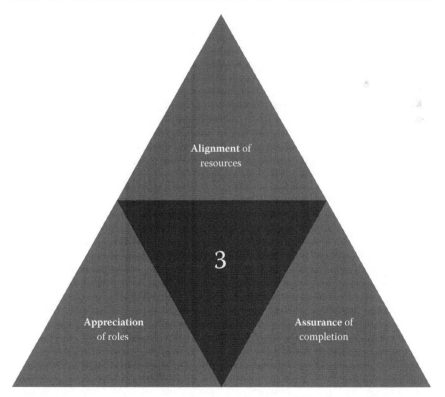

FIGURE 5.1
A^3 change realization model.

of such waste demonstrates a lack of alignment; people without a sense of priority, without a clear appreciation of what matters most and how their work must support those priorities, will struggle to manage their time well. As a result, they will be less effective.

Applying the system discussed here, then, has the goal of resolving those gaps, helping people understand not only where we are going, but also how they can help get the organization to that destination.

The mechanics of the system itself build off the frameworks presented in previous chapters, as indicated. The strategy roadmap and the value map together form the foundation for the operating plan, collectively represented in Figure 5.2. The strategy roadmap and value map provide perspective, organize our thoughts, and give us customer and business insights that are simple, clear, and repeatable, but not yet actionable until we put them in the form of the operating plan.

In this approach, you will recall from Chapters 3 and 4, the gaps illustrated in the value map are articulated in Box C of the strategy roadmap, as the arrow in Figure 5.2 highlights. The bullet statements in Box B of the roadmap are expanded upon to form the foundation of the operating plan; that is, the firm discusses who they are and where they are going at the top of the operating plan. Making these statements twice during the planning process may seem redundant, but appreciate again the purpose of the tools. The roadmap gathers the firm's thoughts and expresses them in a single page—this is who we are, where we are going, some of the obstacles we face, and the basic tactics that will move us toward our goals. While that single page is critical in forcing a simple and clear understanding of the firm's situation, it will be insufficient in detail and scope for the firm to be able to execute anything meaningfully and reliably. The value map then compares our current state to what we believe current and future customers want, paving the way for the project bullets expressed in the lower portion of the roadmap, although again lacking actionable detail.

The operating plan is actionable. When completed in sufficient depth, it can run up to 15 or 20 pages in many organizations. It summarizes again who the organization is and where they are going, and then *maps out the work and projects associated with achieving that plan in enough detail* that it behaves much like a recipe for the firm's leadership. I was introduced to an operating plan almost 20 years ago by a man named Brian Allenspach when I got to know an organization called Meridian Technologies in Michigan. Operating plans are still one of my favorite execution tools today.

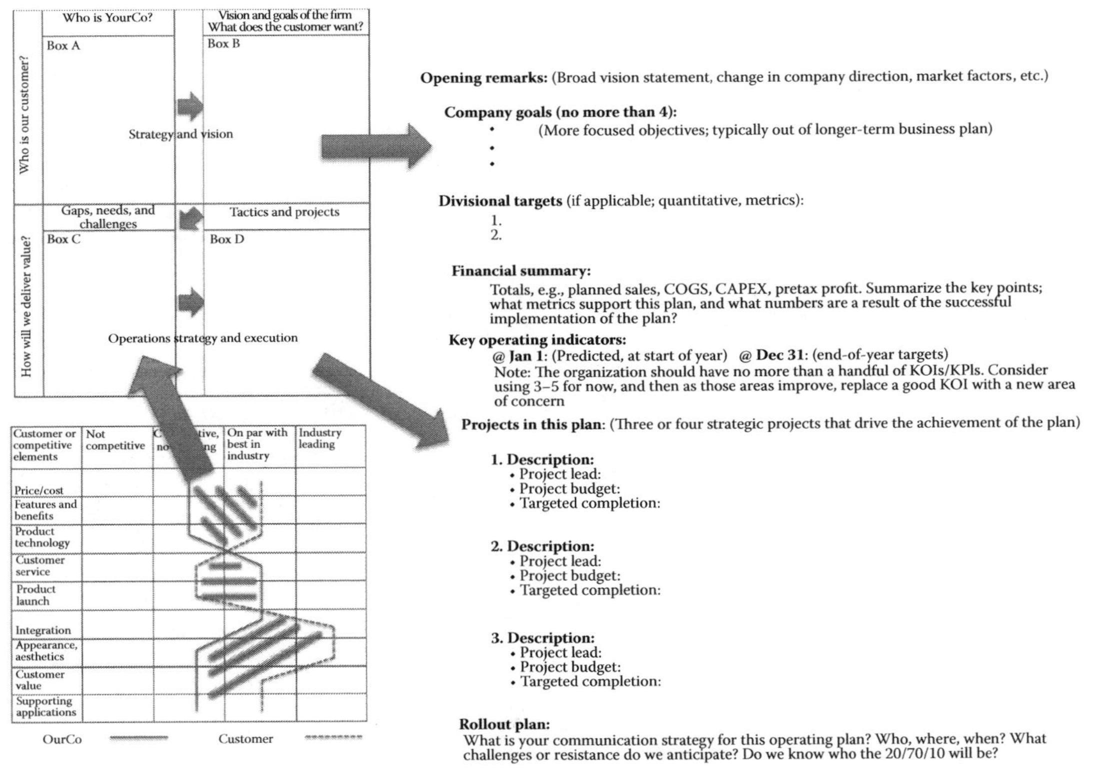

Opening remarks: (Broad vision statement, change in company direction, market factors, etc.)

Company goals (no more than 4):
- (More focused objectives; typically out of longer-term business plan)
-
-

Divisional targets (if applicable; quantitative, metrics):
1.
2.

Financial summary:

Totals, e.g., planned sales, COGS, CAPEX, pretax profit. Summarize the key points; what metrics support this plan, and what numbers are a result of the successful implementation of the plan?

Key operating indicators:

@ Jan 1: (Predicted, at start of year)   @ Dec 31: (end-of-year targets)

Note: The organization should have no more than a handful of KOIs/KPIs. Consider using 3–5 for now, and then as those areas improve, replace a good KOI with a new area of concern

Projects in this plan: (Three or four strategic projects that drive the achievement of the plan)

1. Description:
- Project lead:
- Project budget:
- Targeted completion:

2. Description:
- Project lead:
- Project budget:
- Targeted completion:

3. Description:
- Project lead:
- Project budget:
- Targeted completion:

Rollout plan:

What is your communication strategy for this operating plan? Who, where, when? What challenges or resistance do we anticipate? Do we know who the 20/70/10 will be?

Who is YourCo?	Vision and goals of the firm What does the customer want?
Box A	Box B

Strategy and vision

Gaps, needs, and challenges	Tactics and projects
Box C	Box D

Operations strategy and execution

Who is our customer?

How will we deliver value?

	Not competitive	Competitive, not leading	On par with best in industry	Industry leading
Customer or competitive elements				
Price/cost				
Features and benefits				
Product technology				
Customer service				
Product launch				
Integration				
Appearance, aesthetics				
Customer value				
Supporting applications				

OurCo ————   Customer ▪▪▪▪▪▪▪▪

FIGURE 5.2

Framework relationships.

I will take a few moments here to clarify some common terminology. Most organizations have a business plan, or perhaps what they may call their strategic plan. Often created with a three- to five-year scope, the business plan is a detailed vision statement of where the firm is going over the next several years. It can discuss current operations, customers, and competitors, and include financial statements and the general state of the union. There can be significant value to the firm in creating this business plan, but for most firms, the results do not justify the effort and work involved. The investment in resources and time to create the plan often outweighs the utility the firm gets from the plan. Many firms find they rarely look at the business plan after spending hundreds of man-hours and significant expense building it. The other problem with traditional business plans is the time frame. Detailed plans are made, intended to be developed to fruition over a period of three to five years, when in many industries the assumptions and conditions that go into those plans are obsolete within a year. All that effort, and the plan is no longer relevant. Management guru Henry Mintzberg was a fan of saying that in the time it takes to develop, analyze, finalize, and publish a business plan, it's out of date.

THE OPERATING PLAN

An operating plan, on the other hand, is intended for the next 12 months, specifically the organization's upcoming fiscal year. Effective operating plans are a balance of serving today's customers and building the capability to excite the customers of tomorrow. Operations are tuned, and refined to improve current processes and services; quality is improved and defects are reduced or eliminated; incremental enhancements are implemented. Components of the plan focused on current customers are intended to increase the organization's ability to *capture value* from today's operations. At the same time, preparations for tomorrow's customer are underway. In this way, the operating plan also outlines projects and initiatives that *create value* for new customers, or value for existing customers in new ways. For both customers, those of today and tomorrow, the key initiatives and projects summarized in the operating plan define the work we are expecting the organization to complete within the next 12 months.

Several themes here are worth discussing further. Some experts will advocate that new initiatives and projects (the work associated with tomorrow's customers) should be separate from current initiatives. That is, the operating plan should look after today's customers, while a strategic plan will guide the firm toward supporting tomorrow's customers. While I understand why that perspective exists, I disagree with the approach for several reasons. First, there are often common resources within the firm supporting both current operations and future projects. Second, any time we have two separate planning activities, we run the risk of communication shortfalls and blunders, where the right people do not have all the information they need. Third, building the operating plan to include both time frames highlights the importance of supporting both customer groups effectively. Finally, the real goal of constructing the plan this way is to increase the visibility, priority, and awareness of key work the organization needs to get done in the next 12 months, thus better enabling the execution of that work. As I have said, at the end of the day, our customers are buying our execution, and not much else.

The other key point associated with a 12-month operating plan is the time frame itself. Within a 12-month window, we can expect some elements of the plan to change. Economic assumptions, energy prices, the availability of a key piece of technology—something within our plan will not turn out quite the way we had anticipated. As leaders, we are aware of this, and that is the purpose of the application of risk management within our planning activities. More importantly, we also know that more of our assumptions—the majority of the plan, in fact—will be valid over a 12-month period than in a traditional 3- or 5-year business plan.

The final part of this discussion relates to accountability. That 12-month cycle obviously relates directly to our fiscal year. By increasing the visibility, priority, and awareness of the work and projects associated with the operating plan, we are making a commitment to all stakeholders (employees, shareholders, customers, and the community at large) that this is what we will accomplish next year. The communication, support, execution, and follow-up of the plan, then, all need to align to ensure we do what we say. In this way, the operating plan behaves like an organizational contract.

You will recall we started Chapter 1 with several questions: Do you know what the most important use of your time is today? Do people within the firm know which projects are more important than others? Do you wake up in the morning with a clear sense of purpose? It has admittedly taken us some time to get to where we have answers to those questions, but that is the substance of the operating plan, and it, more than any of the other tools here, creates the culture of agility and execution we seek in the

A³—the alignment of resources, the appreciation of roles, and the assurance of completion. While the roadmap and value map are constructed during the planning process for the firm, they are not reviewed to any significant extent during the organization's fiscal year. They may be reviewed, discussed, or used to support a presentation and tell the firm's "story," but they are essentially static, having "done their job" in the construction of an operating plan. The operating plan itself becomes a management tool within the firm to ensure the organization is tracking toward its goals.

Let's fill in some of the blanks currently associated with building an effective operating plan. The top portion of the plan—business and divisional goals and objectives, including the big opportunity—comes from the top of the strategy roadmap, and should be a blend of objectives for both the next 12 months and a longer-term look into the future. Immediately below those broad statements are a series of numbers—these are financial and operating indicators that relate to the upcoming fiscal year alone. Tables 5.1 and 5.2 are examples of what we might see in those sections.

TABLE 5.1

ECHS Operating Plan Financials

Description	Amount
Projected Annual Revenue, Ticket Sales	$1,100,000
Project Annual Revenue, Merchandise	$125,000
Current # Guests, Oct/Nov	1500
Current Revenue, Oct/Nov Ticket Sales	$23,000
Current Revenue, Oct/Nov Merchandise	$4000
Thanksgiving Project CAPEX	$260,000
Marketing Expenses	$20,000
Project Launch Expenses	$30,000
Total, Thanksgiving Project	$310,000
Projected Guests, Oct/Nov	20,000
Projected Revenue, Ticket and Merchandise, Oct/Nov	$300,000

TABLE 5.2

ECHS Key Operating Indicators

Key Operating Indicator Description
Monthly attendance, year over year
Website hits, before and after Thanksgiving project
One-time ticket conversions to membership sales

This data represents a firm we will call East Coast Historical Society (ECHS), a not-for-profit organization that operates a number of facilities of, obviously, historical significance. These sites attract both tourists and students of history, and are representative of the lives and existence of some of the earliest European settlers to North America. The challenge ECHS faces is the cyclicality in its "business"—tourists and travelers flock to its attractions throughout the summer months, but numbers drop significantly by early October. This cyclicality results in both financial strain and operational burdens to the organization. Think employee retention in this type of operation—employee knowledge is fundamental to tour operations, yet 80% of employees leave after the summer is over, many not returning the following year.

Instead of just accepting the current state of affairs, ECHS leadership asks an important question: How can we reduce the cyclicality of the business? This is the society's big opportunity. More specifically, how could we attract a meaningful number of guests, say, in the fall? This discussion leads to the suggestion that ECHS creates an interactive and historically set Thanksgiving supper event, held five nights per week for a month (represented in Table 5.1 as Oct/Nov, in recognition that Canadians celebrate Thanksgiving a month earlier than Americans). Not only is the dinner intended to be a fun night out, but the event will attract locals, many of which have not visited ECHS facilities since they were children. Assuming the event is executed well, these fall guests may want to return again the following summer for historical tours, resulting in ancillary benefits from the new Thanksgiving project.

There may be a few other key operating indicators (KOIs) ECHS tracks through the year, but the purpose of highlighting these particular metrics in the operating plan is that they will measure the impact of the new initiative (Table 5.2). It is important to point out that we resist the urge as leadership to track too many metrics. KOIs, by definition, are the key numbers we need to have daily or weekly visibility of, in managing our operations. Thought leader Michael Hammer stated that he "scarcely ever" encounters (an organization) that believes it has an effective set of metrics.[1] In fact, the widespread consensus is that we measure too much or too little. Building on our discussion of seven from earlier, my own experience suggests the following guidelines in the application of your KOIs:

- Fewer is better. Keep the KOIs to no more than six or seven key metrics. Too many and you lose sight of what is important, or it takes too long to generate or even review the numbers, so we don't do it.

- Maintain your priority. The KOIs need to reflect what is most important in your operations right now. If we have solved a problem, or the project launched six months ago, stop tracking that number and focus elsewhere. Move on!
- Keep it visible; keep it simple. Make it easy for people whose job relies on the numbers to see the numbers. Get them up on a whiteboard near the operation or in a high traffic area of the firm. Expensive technology is not always required. A public pool in British Columbia tracks the number of deaths by drowning in the province, along with the number of days since the last drowning, on a whiteboard as people walk into the pool. This is certainly effective in encouraging swimmers to be smart while they enjoy the pool.
- Connect rewards to goals. When KOIs are satisfied within your operations, reward people accordingly, reinforcing organizational commitment to goals and vision.

In the case of ECHS, it is interested in the impact and interest in its new Thanksgiving project. Measurement of website traffic before and after it announces the new attraction will capture short-term appeal, and the conversion of one-time tickets to annual members of ECHS will give them a sense of increasing overall interest in the society itself.

Below the financials and KOIs in the operating plan are the key projects the organization needs to focus on over the next 12 months. I commented earlier that projects noted in Box D of the strategy roadmap are not sufficient in detail in that framework to really be actionable; here is where we provide that level of detail. We will stay with the example of the ECHS within this discussion. The projects we outline in the operating plan should take up roughly a quarter to half page of space each—not so little that we cannot understand what we need to know about the project, but not so much that we are repeating all the information in the project plan itself. This is intended to be leadership-level information on priority initiatives within the organization. Look for

- Project title and description: A one- to two-sentence outline of the key elements of the project.
- Project lead or sponsor: This is not the project manager, but the executive-level sponsor who effectively owns the project. This person does not manage the project day to day, but enables it, endorses it, and makes sure the project continues to get the priority it needs.

The sponsor can also speak to the project effectively among his or her peers during monthly executive operating plan reviews (more on this later).

- Target completion: The most important element of timing for the project at the leadership level is whether we are actually on time. This can be a hard date or something broader, like 3Q17 (third quarter, 2017).
- Project budget: The total investment associated with this project, including necessary capital and expenses (these can be listed separately if preferred).

For the ECHS, a couple of the projects in support of its Thanksgiving initiative might look like this:*

Project Description: Thanksgiving facilities
Develop a floor plan for the Thanksgiving event within the courtyard, including tables, staging, and an open area for dancing. Project includes the acquisition of any necessary period-appropriate fixtures and furnishings to support the event.
Project lead: Events director, ECHS
Target completion: August 31, 2018
Project budget: $260,000

Project description: Thanksgiving marketing
As this is a new event, this project will build the awareness and enthusiasm for the Thanksgiving project. Activities include local promotion, social media, and appeal to long-term members and advocates for ECHS activities.
Project lead: Marketing director, ECHS
Target completion: September 30, 2018
Project budget: $20,000

It is important to point out here that an operating plan is a management tool to be applied at the executive level of the organization. Project descriptions are a few sentences that provide leadership with the basic information they need to understand the scope of the project; project leads are the sponsors at their level of the firm. This level of project visibility within the organization has a number of advantages. Key projects outlined in the

---

* Appendix B provides a more complete example of an operating plan for the ECHS.

plan, both those supporting current operations and future initiatives, will have to more closely support the vision and strategy of the organization. An initiative that does not "fit" will stand out like a sore thumb.

Executive sponsors on projects both support their project and are responsible for reporting on that project at the leadership level of the firm. That dual role ensures ongoing commitment to the project, avoiding the potential for a project to be orphaned and fail in its execution.

The operating plan becomes a foundation for communication and follow-up within the organization. We now have a mechanism that illustrates both our direction and strategy, and the projects and work associated with delivering that strategy. "This is our strategy, and more importantly, here is your role in bringing that strategy to life." Follow-up itself is a function of management style and culture within the firm, but I would like to suggest that the management group holds operating plan meetings at least monthly, especially in the early days of a new plan. Choose a common day every month (e.g., third Thursday afternoon), and have the managers and execs book that period into their calendar every month. This group could be 10–20 people in some firms, which can get unwieldy, but the group will settle into a rhythm within a month or two. Plan to spend 5–10 minutes on each key project: Where do we stand? What do you need? Will anything get in the way of timely launch? If a project is getting off track, this is the time to prioritize and reallocate resources within the firm to make sure we launch well. One could imagine that delaying the Thanksgiving project two months at ECHS would be disastrous—who wants to celebrate Thanksgiving in December?

The collective efforts of building and executing the operating plan move the organization toward the state embodied in the A^3—aligned resources, appreciation of roles, and assurance of completion. You have likely heard the phrase "No one gets credit for fixing problems before they happen"; while we smile when we hear something like that, our agile culture is really the antithesis of that statement. How do we hold people accountable if we cannot connect their day-to-day responsibilities to customer value? Building the operating plan and communicating that plan to the organization can be considered sharpening the axe. Executing the plan is cutting the wood.

While we represent the three A's in the A^3 as equal, it would be fair to say that *alignment of resources* has to take priority in both our planning activities and the actual launch of the plan at the start of the year. As part of our discussion in Chapter 3, we discussed the idea that strategy is the decision of both what the firm does and does not do. As an organization, we cannot be all things to all people—any attempt to do that results in failure or mediocrity. Within the firm, then, alignment is the ability of the firm to focus on work that matters in delivering that strategy and creating value for our customers. Doing more of the work that matters results in doing less work that doesn't matter. This again circles back to our Lean and agile philosophy.

Another phrase I often use is "People can't do what they don't understand." While this may sound like motherhood, and obvious, think about how often people struggle not only with a new initiative itself, but also with why they are doing it. This is the value of effective communication of our plan, creating an *appreciation of roles*. Teams that can connect their work to organizational vision work faster, feel better about that work, and are better able to prioritize activities given the typical constraints of day-to-day business. We are effectively looking the team in the eye, seeing them nod, and saying, "Yes, I've got this."

When applied to current operations, management involvement, and engagement, this perspective leads, on average, to reductions in inventory by 20%, fewer defects by half, and improved output by 10%.[2] When A.G. Lafley took over as CEO at Proctor & Gamble in 2000, for example, he witnessed a lack of personal accountability within the executive ranks for both new initiatives and current operations. He instituted a weekly follow-up process where execs reported on any missed deliverables, right down to missing cases of product scheduled for shipment to customers, and what that executive was doing to correct the matter. Within a few months, missing and late product fell below 1%.[3] Including current operations in the operating plan ensures we don't swing too far toward new projects and compromise our existing customers. Compare this with Rick Wagoner's approach at General Motors, discussed in Chapter 3, and we see a stark contrast.

The final A here is the *assurance of completion*. One of Mike Tyson's more memorable quotes tied planning and execution together nicely— "Everyone has a plan 'til they get punched in the mouth," which was likely a derivative of Helmuth Von Molke's more eloquent version: "No plan survives contact with the enemy." Building effective and realistic plans themselves is crucial, and communicating and understanding those plans is equally important, but the moment we launch, life happens. The behavior within the organization is the final leg of the stool that brings execution to the forefront of importance. This component of the discussion relates to your ability to rely on your peers, their ability to rely on you, and having the systems in place to support the completion of work and tasks around the organization.

Execution is more than just sticking to the plan. Your ability to count on a team member or colleague in executing a plan prevents a "host of dysfunctional behaviors,"[4] according to MIT professor Don Sull. For example, customer deliverables can slip, and managers duplicate efforts and may delay or pass on potentially lucrative opportunities. Gamesmanship and turf issues can often arise as well, as most of us have seen. The situation may be worse still when execution within the organization is reliant on a single individual or CEO—what happens when that CEO retires or moves on to other opportunities? Here, after the organization gets comfortable and familiar with the application of the operating plan, and the processes of building and following up on the plan are embedded, the firm is in a far better position to sustain its momentum even with the loss of key individuals. This is the dual need for both effective planning and structure in the organization.

Execution-driven organizational structures have a number of common elements:

- They are flat, eliminating unnecessary levels that often have the effect of slowing down communication or having elements of the plan lost in the translation. How many levels of vice president does your firm have? Many banks, for example, have vice presidents, senior vice presidents, and executive vice presidents. Who is doing the real work? Zappos, the online shoe and clothing retailer, on the other hand, has seen the benefit of flattening its organization. Employees feel empowered, are solving problems more quickly, and are more engaged and productive. Customers see the benefits through a faster response and improved customer service.[5]
- Roles and responsibilities are clear, with an absence of ambiguity in titles and functions. Firms with chief talent officers, chief agility officers, chief diversity officers, or chief sustainability officers likely have too many people in the C-suite,* and suffer from a lack of clarity when compared with their peers with human resources (HR) directors and chief operating officers.

---

* Real titles in real firms, folks, and yes, very much over the top in my opinion. See "The C-Suite Gets Crowded," *Canadian Business*, April 2015.

- Customers are at the center of both strategy and structure within the firm. This is a tenant of design thinking,* where the organization's operations are focused on customer value, user needs, and experiences.[6]
- The role of corporate staff and administration in the firm is to support the frontline, customer-facing operations. Your customers really are not interested in paying for head office, so make sure the business is structured so those resources add value by making frontline workers more effective. In the United Kingdom, for example, many public school systems are centralizing administrative and HR tasks to relieve principals (their head teachers) of those duties. The revised model will enable the head teachers to capitalize on their many more years of experience and apply those skills in the development of the junior teachers on their staff.[7]

This chapter is about action, the work embarked on by the firm in pursuit of its strategy. When that work is aligned to goals and our people are focused on the outcome, time seems to slow down and more is accomplished. Objectives are met, value is created, and customers smile. The firm is becoming agile.

ONE LAST STORY

I once flew from Toronto to the United States for the Production and Operations Management Society's annual conference, where I was presenting a case study and chairing a research panel. While booking my ticket online some time earlier, I noted that I had the opportunity to buy a one-time pass for the airline's executive lounge the day of my flight. Unsure of my schedule for the day of my departure, I filed the information for later use if some time opened up.

The day of the trip, my morning meeting wrapped up earlier than expected in Toronto, so I headed for the airport expecting to be able to buy a pass for the lounge and get some work done prior to the flight. Sadly,

---

* Design thinking is at its core an innovation and problem-solving process, where the party defines its problem, considers options, analyzes and selects the most appropriate option, and then implements that solution. Repeat as necessary. Tim Brown and Roger Martin are pioneers in this area, and I am a big fan of the method, using it with both students and clients in situational case analysis.

I was informed by the hostess for the lounge that one-time passes are only available online when you buy your ticket. Checking with the customer service desk in the concourse (admittedly, I can be stubborn), I got the same response. This representative, however, kindly referred me to an independent lounge down the hall where I could purchase a pass for the afternoon. Problem solved.

Offering the service online but not in person creates ill will. While this is an unsatisfactory situation for the consumer, the "glass is half full" people would view this as an opportunity for innovation. Airlines are cyclical businesses, and financial struggles, customer loyalty, and enthusiasm by nature go through peaks and valleys. In such an environment, any source of new ideas should be treasured, especially those that (1) enhance satisfaction, (2) potentially increase customer loyalty, and (3) are easy to implement. Many firms have internal suggestion programs, while others benchmark for best-in-class tactics. Both are good programs when run well and new ideas get off the ground quickly and on a regular basis.

In this case, I wonder if the airline's representatives were noting my request as an opportunity. Given the comment I overheard as I walked away ("another guy trying to buy a pass for the lounge"), I somehow doubt it. These unsolicited inputs are not typically tracked or, worse, recorded. Many service firms don't often *really listen* to their customers.

How valuable could this process be to the airline? Let's say the hostess noted my query and asked internally, "Why *don't* we do this?" Responsive, progressive leadership within the premium services department of the airline that is responsible for the lounge says, "Let's try it." Pricing of, say, $40 per day is implemented (I paid about $45 at the independent lounge), and the unsolicited idea is implemented within weeks (sure, it could be done in days in other industries, but this is an airline). Experiment with the concept in Toronto or Vancouver first, and if it works, get it out there. To alleviate concerns with lounge crowding or capacity, limit the number of on-site day passes available.

The benefits? A satisfied customer, incremental revenue for the airline, and a differentiator from the other big airline in Canada that doesn't have lounges (yet). Some other related services could be natural extensions of this idea as well. As it is right now, the airline has created a negative experience for at least one of its customers.

Many organizations don't have the resources or structure to support product or service research and development (R&D), especially in the current economy. In this environment, organizational culture needs to support the collection and capture of novel ideas with innovative opportunities, wherever the ideas come from. Effective, Lean firms gather these ideas, refine them, and get them out in front of the customer in a hurry, regardless of the climate.

REFERENCES

1. Hammer, M. The 7 deadly sins of performance measurement (and how to avoid them). *MIT Sloan Management Review*, Spring 2007, p. 19.
2. Bloom, N., Sadun, R., and Van Reenen, J. Does management really work? *Harvard Business Review*, November 1, 2012, p. 79.
3. Simons, R. *Seven Strategy Question*. Watertown, MA: HBR Press, 2010, p. 85. Lafley, A.G., and Charan, R. *The Game-Changer*. New York: Crown Business, 2008, chapters 1 and 2.
4. Sull, D. Why strategy execution unravels—And what to do about it. *Harvard Business Review*, March 2015, p. 61.
5. Bosanac, A. Get flatter. *Canadian Business*, October 2015, p. 46.
6. Kolko, J. Design thinking comes of age. *Harvard Business Review*, September 2015, p. 4.
7. Hancock, B., and Ellsworth, D. Redesigning knowledge work. *Harvard Business Review*, January–February 2013, p. 60.

6

Lean Innovation

We demand rigidly defined areas of doubt and uncertainty!

Douglas Adams

I'm lousy with names, so all my best friends since childhood have been named Rob. Keep it simple.

In 1968, at the Olympic Games in Mexico City, American Dick Fosbury set a new Olympic record in the high jump, winning the gold medal with a jump of 7 feet 4.25 inches. The most interesting part of the story is that Fosbury may never have attained the status of a world-class athlete had he not created his own style of jumping, the *Fosbury flop*.

People around sports, and especially track and field, have heard of, or even practiced the Fosbury flop, as that style of jumping has become the quintessential method for maximizing a jumper's height over the bar. Growing up, however, Fosbury was a questionable athlete at best. Despite his height (he topped 6 feet 4 inches at an early age), he was admittedly a mediocre basketball player and a worse football player. He enjoyed sports though, and kept looking. His circuitous route to the high jump still did not initially lead to promising results. Jumpers at the time were using the straddle technique, where the jumper crosses the bar facing down, essentially rolling sideways before landing on the mat. Despite his height, Fosbury could barely jump 5 feet 4 inches, and knew he had to try something different.

He asked his coach if he could experiment with the scissors approach, where the athlete approaches the bar from the side and scissors one leg and then the other over the top. Not sensing greatness, but at the same time not wanting to dampen Fosbury's enthusiasm, the coach said to try whatever he wanted and moved on to another group of athletes. With the scissors technique, the maximum height a jumper will achieve is roughly the height he or she can elevate their hips to. Fosbury quickly realized that unless he could do something to raise his hips further, he was as bad off as with the straddle. On subsequent jumps, he threw his hips higher and higher, with an unintended consequence of dropping his shoulders and traveling backwards over the bar while facing up. Suddenly, he was jumping new personal bests 6 inches higher than with the scissors or straddle. This was 1963.[1]

Two years later, he was a student athlete at Oregon State University, winning meets and yet attracting as many curious looks as applause for his success. The looks and the laughs wore on Fosbury, and he considered moving back to the straddle. His coach, however, realized Fosbury was clearing heights of 6 feet 6 inches by a large margin, and knew he had a jumper. Over the next couple of years, Fosbury refined his technique, now nicknamed the "flop" for its blind, falling-backwards-in-water look, moving his takeoff point farther from the bar for greater heights, kicking his legs up as they approached the bar, and tucking his arms out of the way. Although he won many meets while in college, he was ranked only 61st in the world by the time he secured the third and final place for high jump on the U.S. Olympic team in 1968.

As the heights went increasingly higher the day of his event, Fosbury began to stand out. By the time the height was 2.20 m (7 feet 3 inches), he had not missed a jump yet, while only two other jumpers were still alive in the competition. He won the gold medal with a jump of 2.24 m (7 feet 4.25 inches).

While a number of other jumpers were experimenting with other jumping styles, it was Fosbury's gold that gained global notoriety and, more importantly, credibility for the flop. Just four years later at the 1972 Munich Olympics, 28 of the 40 athletes competing in the high jump were using the Fosbury flop, and since 1976, no Olympic jumper has won the high jump using any other technique.

I like to say that good leaders have three characteristics: they recognize opportunities, they avoid catastrophes, and they break paradigms. In Fosbury's case, he knew he had to take a completely different approach, as the current method of jumping had proved unsuccessful. He could continue to compete using the straddle or scissors, but he would lose, or potentially fail to even make the team. In developing his own approach, tuning, refining, and adapting as he flew higher, he changed the way we play the game. In effect, he changed the way the market behaves and competes.

This chapter is about connecting our theme of agility and simplicity with innovation. It is not, however, a "how-to" approach to innovation.* We will correct some of the myths about innovation, while taking a different perspective on what innovation really means and why it is a crucial part of any organization's strategy. The key element for us here is that even fast-moving agile firms need to take a balanced approach, serving today's customers effectively while finding a path to look after the customer of tomorrow.

Would you consider yourself an innovative or creative person? This can be a challenging question. Executives, managers, and students I work with, when posed this question, as a majority respond in the negative. Fewer people than naught consider themselves creative, or believe they work in innovative organizations. There are usually several reasons for this: the first is that people are often too busy to be creative. The projects, day job, customers, meetings, and email associated with their work are too hectic to allow time to be more creative—they simply believe they don't have time.

This is one of the reasons I have coupled Lean and innovation over the years—as we have discussed, an outcome of the Lean initiative in the firm is the availability of more time to focus on the work that matters most. Less complexity, less waste, and less non-value-added activity mean we have more time, which can be applied here in new and creative ways. The other key advantage of a Lean approach to innovation is that no research and development (R&D) lab is required. Innovation can occur in any firm, but more on this in a moment.

Another reason people don't view themselves as innovative is that they feel their industry or business may not require innovation—there has been little structural change in the industry in years, or (shudder) the firm holds the dominant position in their space, and has little to fear from competitors. We will tackle this position as well in the coming pages.

The final reason people do not feel creative or innovative is a narrow perspective of what innovation is, where most often it is associated with creative roles within the firm—the designers, engineers, thought leaders, or others who do that type of work. Innovation is the responsibility of *that*

---

* Please see my first book, best-selling *Lean Innovation: Understanding What's Next in Today's Economy* (CRC Press, 2012), for a more in-depth look at innovation.

group of people, not me and not my department. This perspective is perhaps the largest single opportunity for us as an organization, but in fact, we will debunk all three of these innovation myths here and help you as a leader put a priority on creative thinking across the organization, whether you are in government, practice health care or education, run a service organization, or are building technology for the coming electric car boom. We all have a responsibility to drive "next" in our roles, departments, and firms.

The right place to start may be with a clear sense of what it means to be innovative. Our first thoughts with innovation typically surround new technology. Those electric cars from Tesla. Wearable technology. The Internet of Things (IoT) (I have mixed thoughts on this one—more later). Biomedical devices, drug therapies, and medical implants. Commercial space travel and drone technologies. These are all product-based innovations coming out of R&D labs with research budgets in the millions and billions of dollars. They are all important to society, and we rely heavily on the firms driving this development activity, but such work is also not within the wheelhouse of most organizations. Does that mean the rest of us cannot be innovative? Nothing could be further from the truth. In fact, for the rest of us, innovation relies far less on the expensive and time-consuming heavy lifting associated with typical innovation, and for many people, they are driving innovation and change within their operations without realizing it.

Those opportunities I speak of are in the realm of service and process innovation. Anytime we improve a process—reduce complexity, enhance response time, or eliminate downtime—we are innovating that process. Lean and innovation together again. Process innovation often results in an improved outcome for our customers, or a service innovation. When we consider the vast number of processes across our organizations, many of which deserve another look in the interest of agility, we can agree that essentially all of our employees and departments have some level of responsibility to be innovative. *You own that process! Don't complain about it; fix it!* Process innovation can lead to product innovation as well and, ultimately on a grander scale, business model innovation, what we are responsible for as leadership. Some of our work in Chapter 4, then, will foster and drive innovation.

Under the watch of CEO Mark Parker, Nike has evolved its development processes and aligned the organization to a "category offense" approach away from traditional footwear and apparel streams.[2] What started with design teams focusing on, say, basketball as a category, rather than shoe designers focusing on just the shoe, resulted in a new approach to manufacturing configurations and marketing strategies, and ultimately the category offense on basketball. This seems like a simple premise—consider the athlete or customer as an entity, not just a buyer of footwear. How do we then design a system or package for the customer and get closer to being the sole source for their basketball needs? The business model has evolved and gone further downstream as a result, leading to hundreds of new Nike brand stores where the category specialists can focus on the full package for even the weekend or part-time athlete. Nike's website (http://www.nike.com) enables both approaches for its online shoppers, supporting traditional customers with *Shoes* and *Clothing* headers, and the category view with a *Shop by Sport* header.

Rubbermaid, on the other hand, struggled with this customer centricity in the early 1990s. Under CEO Wolfgang Schmidt, Rubbermaid's strategy was to "bury [their] competition under such a profusion of products they couldn't copy [Rubbermaid]."[3] The company quickly grew to more than 5000 stock keeping units (SKUs) sourced from thousands of suppliers, including more than 400 colors and even 18 shades of black (how many shades of grey is unclear at this time). Their supply chain became unwieldy, resin prices increased with the price of oil, and pressure from customers like Wal-Mart prevented them from passing along price increases. Their product proliferation strategy was a lot of things, but none of them were simple, customer focused, or easily managed by the organization. Rubbermaid abandoned that strategy in 1995, reducing its portfolio by half and focusing on the products and colors customers wanted most. Schmidt left in 1999 when Rubbermaid was purchased by Newall Companies.

ANATOMY OF A CURVE

One of my favorite methods of enabling an innovation discussion is a look at the life cycle* curve (Figure 6.1). I am of the opinion that the life cycle

---

* This is often referred to as a product life cycle, under the mistaken perspective that the curve is the sole domain of product or manufacturing organizations. We will show here how it also applies to services and, in fact, business models—hence the abbreviated, but more comprehensive title.

represented here is a law, much like gravity, and that French toast must only be made with white bread, in that all organizations, products, services, and business models are governed by the dynamics of this curve. Everything that is born will die, and every business concept that is conceived, refined, and launched will one day be made obsolete, without exception.

Let's start with a look at a single life cycle curve in isolation, and understand more about the anatomy of that curve. Figure 6.1 illustrates the growth of a product or service, with terms most of us are familiar with. The curve presents the inception, growth, maturity, and eventual demise of that product or service. We could consider Blockbuster Video as an example, conceived as a service that consolidated and brought mainstream access to thousands of movie titles for millions of households across North America. As it implemented its strategy of having a store located within 15 minutes of 75% of the population, access and volume (in titles available,

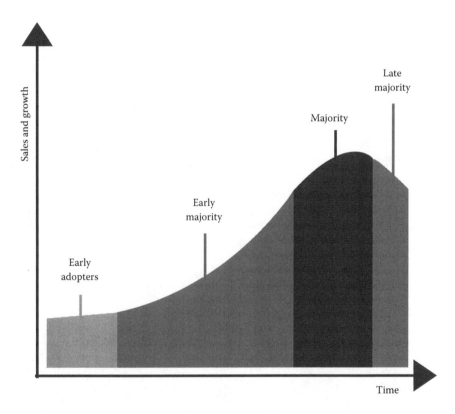

FIGURE 6.1
Life cycle.

rental customers, revenue, and profit) all soared. As Netflix entered the movie rental business with a completely new model, Blockbuster's model matured and the chain eventually disappeared.

Look now to Figure 6.2. Early in a new service or business model, leadership should be most concerned with the exploration of new ideas and innovative approaches to creating value for their customers. As those ideas develop and are brought to life or commercialized, the urgency shifts to the exploitation of that idea and capturing volume and the value potential within the idea. It is important to stress the difference here between creativity and innovation—ideas are essential, but by themselves create no tangible value for the firm or its customers. Until the idea is commercialized, patented, or implemented within the firm, that idea is not innovation. Innovation is the idea brought to life. Put more bluntly, it is not innovation if you don't get paid.[4]

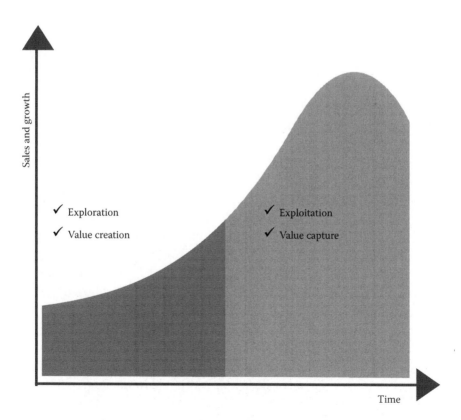

FIGURE 6.2
What leadership needs to think about.

This concept of *value capture* is an often-overlooked element; essentially, it is the execution of an idea (perhaps a good position to refresh your team on the ideas presented in Chapter 5). One of the most effective approaches leadership can take here is the alignment of the value creation people (the innovators) and the value capture people (the operations or project teams) within the organization. In fact, ideation itself is often more effective if the cross-functional team includes resources responsible for the launch of the idea and those who can think like or for the customer. Don't underestimate the importance of knowing the customers here—in the exploration or value creation phase, the firm needs to connect. The customers that listen here may tell other people within their network (friends, family, blog readers, etc.). Do a good job of this, and *value capture* happens.

WHO IS THE CUSTOMER?

We have discussed the idea of knowing your customer on a number of occasions throughout the book. My purpose in revisiting the concept here is in the interest of focusing our efforts on innovation, and in fact ensuring our innovation efforts pay dividends sooner and to a higher level. Most of us who have been around creativity, ideation, and innovation efforts appreciate that every idea is partially right and partially wrong. That is, every idea needs to be refined before it can be commercialized and yield benefits for some customer.

How are ideas *refined* in your organization? Do you run small-scale pilots, testing an idea or new process internally or with small groups of customers? Do you facilitate thought experiments, or run "what if?" scenarios or sensitivity analysis? A few years ago, McDonald's piloted a new shrimp salad on its menu. While the salads were a hit with customers, further analysis indicated that McDonald's could not actually launch the new menu item broadly across the chain, as there was not enough shrimp available to support anticipated volumes.[5] Some review and anticipation of this dilemma should have taken place prior to the launch of the salad, but that did not happen. While the product was killed shortly after the pilot, it would be interesting to consider whether the chain should have offered it in certain regions only (Gulf Coast states?) or for limited times, while McDonald's secured a sustainable supply of shrimp for larger volumes. Readers are likely aware that shrimp are now being "farmed" inland, far from coastal waters, in places like rural Ontario and central U.S. states, where it is being hailed as the protein source of the future. Sometimes limits imposed are only barriers until leadership finds a way to break that paradigm.

Another angle for our consideration here is the psychology of customer adoption behavior; that is, how do customers *think* when it comes to our service or product? There is some interesting work published in this area by Dilip Soman.[6] Soman points out that many innovations fail as a result of innovators having a flawed understanding of how the end consumer or adopter thinks. For example, where business leaders, policy makers, and developers work under the assumption that customers are rational, value driven, forward looking, and unemotional in their goal to maximize self-interest, behavioral economists now realize that as consumers, we are lazy (physically and cognitively) and tend to rely on our emotion, intuition, and gut-feel in decision making. In other words, organizations may be giving their customers more credit than they deserve. Right or wrong, this highlights the fact that organizations need to spend more time understanding not only their customers' use, utility, or application of their innovation, but really how those customers are thinking while interacting with the service or product itself. At its heart, an innovation should be solving a problem, which enables it to create benefit and value in some form for a customer somewhere. Understanding the psychology of your customer will help the team identify if they are solving the *right* problem.

INNOVATION AND UNINTENDED CONSEQUENCES

Like many teenage boys, our son enjoys the odd video game. We purchased an Xbox 360 system a number of years ago, and in the fall of 2015, he wanted to upgrade to the new Xbox One. We negotiated what portion he would pay, and eventually picked up the new kit. It was a significant amount of money for a "game," so we delayed the purchase for a few weeks to make sure he was serious about it (and to give him a story to tell— "When I was a kid, my parents made me wait three weeks to upgrade our gaming system!"). As you can appreciate, anticipation rose, and when he eventually got the system home, it had to be set up right away so he could give it a test drive.

It turns out the new Xbox One is highly reliant on the Internet and Wi-Fi connectivity to run effectively. In fact, before the system would start up and let him play, it had to download the latest version of its operating system from Microsoft. Now, Microsoft employs some smart people, perhaps some of the smartest people in the Seattle area. This, however, is what one might call cruel and unusual punishment. The software update locked the system up for more than two hours. Picture yourself picking up the new car you just bought, and the dealer telling you the car had to go through a software update, and you would have to wait two hours before driving it away. In our situation, our son just wanted to play. Surely the disc-based game would have worked just fine on the factory-installed version of the system's software.

My colleagues Liana Victorino, Mike Dixon, and Rohit Verma have done some work in the area of the impact of anticipation on service satisfaction. What they found was that in many cases, the effect of anticipation can increase the appreciation of a particular event or service outcome. In this situation, however, the (hopefully) unintended consequences of Microsoft's mandatory upgrade process just created frustration and animosity.*

A fundamental premise of Lean innovation is a reallocation of resources. In some situations, this occurs within the organization, where we dial down waste, inefficiency, or "work" that matters little to our customers in one area of the firm, and move the outcome or benefit of those resources to another area where we can create more value. In other situations, we can create significant new value by combining elements of industry or society in ways that have never been done before. That is, we pull applications, tools, processes, or products from other industries, geographies, or cultures and apply them in new ways for the benefit of our customers. This reallocation of resources is far quicker and less expensive than typical R&D development and innovation. Without some review, testing, and refinement of these ideas, however, we run the risk of such unintended consequences as noted above.

Figure 6.3 is a picture of a small section of my golf bag. The designers developed a pocket with a soft lining, of an appropriate size to hold a wallet, watch, car keys, or perhaps a phone or pair of sunglasses. Given the

---

* We are all likely familiar with a software developer's approach to the almost-ready status at product launch time, necessitating countless updates and upgrades over time, forcing downtime and lost utility on its users.

FIGURE 6.3
Valuables.

cost of these items, their design could thoughtfully protect several hundred dollars or more worth of product. They even labeled the pocket so dummies like me know where to put their stuff.

The seemingly obvious outcome of such a label is that anyone else with potentially more nefarious objectives will know exactly where to look for such valuables. "This is where I keep my cash!" I am sneaky that way, though. I put my wallet in a different pocket. While a somewhat goofy example, this is a situation where there was little or no review of a product between the time it left the design screen and went into production.

From an academic perspective, there have been a number of extremely effective repositioning events, and reallocation of global resources. In these cases, bringing a product from one market to a new market is successful primarily as a result of the product not having any form of serious competition in the new market. You are likely familiar with some of these new product introductions:

- Wild boar: Native to Africa and Eurasia, and introduced to North America as big game animals for hunting. The boar escaped captivity and bred quickly and in quantity. While generally avoiding human contact, boars have still been known to damage crops, root through garbage, and be a general nuisance.
- Asian carp: Native to, well, Asia, the fish was introduced to North American waterways as a filter fish to help clean up commercial ponds. While the method of their escape has not been confirmed,

Asian carp are prolific breeders with incredible jumping ability and now dominate key waterways, such as the Mississippi River, and could wipe out the Great Lakes fishing industry if, and likely when, they appear there.[7]

- Lion fish: Likely introduced to Caribbean and Atlantic coastal waters by aquarium owners (the fish kill and eat any other fish in their aquarium), lion fish are native to the Indo-Pacific region, but are now resident in most reefs between the United States and South America. While very eye catching, lion fish are predatory and carnivorous, and produce up to 30,000 eggs at a time, which drift for hundreds of miles in ocean currents.
- Mysis shrimp: Introduced into Okanagan Lake in the 1960s as a source of food for kokanee (landlocked sockeye salmon), the freshwater shrimp were found to compete with the kokanee for the same food, and are now considered one of the primary reasons for the decline in kokanee fish populations. Efforts to remove the shrimp from the lake commenced in 2009.

Tom Stohlgren, a professor at the University of Waterloo, Ontario, Canada, a leading researcher in the field of biological invasions, calls these situations unwanted foreign organisms (UFOs).[7] Unwanted because the incoming species generally has few, if any, predators in its new domain. Left basically unchecked, the invading species populate and spread at a pace that strips resources from historically native species or consumes those species outright. Where we had distinct continents for millennia, man has figuratively brought the continents together and created a single region with no diversity.

As a species, humanity is often not as smart as we like to think it is.

While interesting, and in many ways very alarming, my core message here is not one of environmental science. Look again at the spread of these species, but with the eye of a Lean innovator. What do these animals have in common in their new environments?

- They are not from around here. They were imported, in business terms, from another market.
- They have no natural competition in their new market, and are changing the way that new market behaves.
- No R&D was necessary for their introduction into the new market. These were not the result of years of research (although arguably,

more research would have been very beneficial and would have perhaps helped society avoid the unintended consequences of these imported species)—the species' new market dominance was simply a repositioning or reallocation of existing resources, a recombination of elements around the environment.

This is the ultimate benefit of a Lean approach to innovation. It focuses on near-term customer needs. When we understand who that customer is, and what they want, refinement and implementation of an idea can be accelerated. The organization can focus on what matters most right now. We understand and can focus more clearly on solving the right problem, and as important, recognize that someone, *somewhere*, has likely solved this problem already. The heavy lifting associated with pure R&D, however beneficial and necessary for society at large, does not need to be our path. We will pursue a recombination of existing elements in society, pulling solutions from other parts of the firm, the industry, or the world where available.

This perspective of innovation and creativity—agile, customer focused, and fast—is a different mindset for many organizations, often necessitating an evolution within the firm's culture. Step 1 is the recognition that innovation needs to be an ongoing process for every organization. Regardless of our industry or position in society, leadership needs to maintain a healthy sense of paranoia: "I'm not crazy; someone really is out to get me!" As I have said before, self-reflection is extremely valuable here as well. Ask the question, if my organization ceased to exist tomorrow, would anyone notice?[8]

Many firms, agencies, institutions, and organizations are perhaps less essential to their customer or society at large than their attitude and behavior justify. As a result, the evolution of their life cycles over the long term looks a lot like what is illustrated in Figure 6.4. Innovation in this firm is not an ongoing process, and leadership fails to appreciate that every business model is subject to the dynamics of the life cycle. Every organization will plateau and stall, and this firm realizes too late that its core product, service, or even business model is becoming obsolete in the eyes of its customer. If the firm is lucky, the market and its own economics enable it to scramble, innovate, and come up with something again appealing to the market. While the organization here survives, the sustainability was not without cost; as the figure indicates, there was a substantial loss in sales, and likely employment, customer enthusiasm, and reputation through the

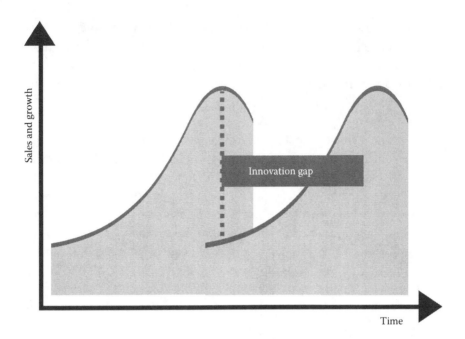

FIGURE 6.4
Innovation gap.

decline of the first curve and the development of the second. I call this lag between life cycles the innovation gap.

Firms such as Harley Davidson, Ford, IBM, and Martin Guitar all encountered the innovation gap when their existing business models plateaued and their companies slid into decline and a "change or die" situation. Waiting too long in these cases resulted in significant pain and effort for the firms in identifying and climbing into the next curve.[9]

It should be pointed out that the relative ease with which the firm starts the next business cycle relies on leadership's ability to recognize that the organization is at the top of the existing curve; that is, that they are currently targeting the "majority" customers who buy on value, price, and convenience, and that this market is about to shrink. In many cases, leadership fails to recognize this situation until too late.

Compare this situation to the firm represented in Figure 6.5. In this organization, innovation is a continuous process. Employees recognize and are rewarded for creativity. Operations serve today's customer, while the organization lays the groundwork to satisfy tomorrow's market.

This firm is agile. An innovation gap still exists, but it is far smaller than in the previous example. In fact, the firm will likely see growth

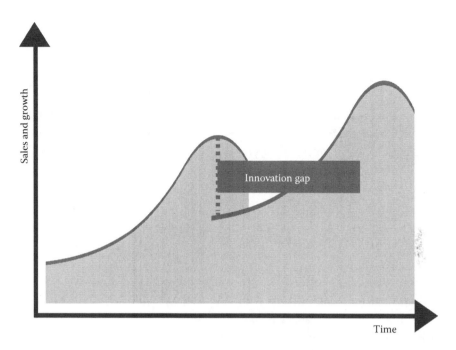

FIGURE 6.5
Innovation gap in an agile firm.

from one business model to the next, based on lessons learned during the previous cycle, skills and employee development, and a stronger sense of what customers are looking for. Think of Figure 6.4 as representative of Blockbuster and Figure 6.5 as Netflix. Figure 6.4 is actually generous in the case of Blockbuster, which started its innovation process too late, trying to enter the online market for DVD rentals, and even considering video on demand (VOD) at a point when it could no longer compete and the market had pivoted. Netflix, on the other hand, started thinking about its next market while it was still growing its current business. One could say that Netflix chose to make itself redundant in the DVD rental market before someone else developed VOD. How many of our organizations would have the courage at the leadership level to take that course?

Netflix's latest initiative is in the actual production of television series and movies, including viewer favorites *House of Cards* and *Orange Is the New Black*. How can we attract more subscribers to our VOD service? Offer them content they cannot get anywhere else. It is fair to say that the spirit of innovation is alive and well at Netflix.

BUSINESS MODEL INNOVATION

When firms like Netflix move from one business model to the next, they demonstrate a progressive evolution as an organization, often shaping their industry as a result. In Figure 6.6, you will note that the next model for Netflix begins well before the previous model has run its course. VOD, for example, was investigated and then initiated while the firm's DVD subscription business was still growing.

Netflix is a great example of a firm with an innovative spirit, and there are a number of others that fit that mold as well (although not as many as there should be). 3M has come a long way from its Minnesota Mining and Manufacturing days. Virgin started off as a record store; shortly, it will be taking people to the edges of space. Corning, the company where the glass is always half full, is 165 years old, surviving multiple economic boom-bust cycles, pivoting and evolving as customers and markets demand something new. Gorilla Glass led to the latest curve for Corning, although it may not have happened had Steve Jobs not required a material for the screen in Apple's iPhone back in 2007.[10] Not only has Corning's product line evolved, but so has its development process. Gone are the days when it took 10 years to produce a new material or application; Corning's teams now produce *next* in six months to a year, demonstrating remarkable agility.

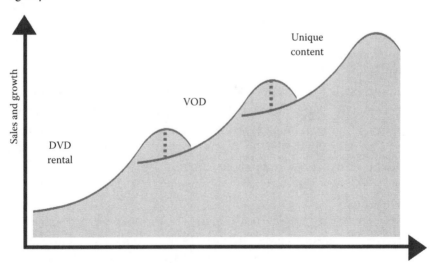

FIGURE 6.6
Netflix business model innovation.

Some organizations do not evolve quickly enough, failing to appreciate the nature of life cycles, or perhaps not recognizing their existing business units are mature. Many leaders blame current economic or other market conditions on declining sales, rather than appreciating that their offering may actually have run its course. Although more than a century old, IBM exhibits these characteristics with surprising consistency, forcing more drastic turnaround efforts as new CEOs step in to right the ship. Through the end of 2014, IBM's revenues had declined for nine straight quarters, a trend that started prior to current CEO Ginni Rometty assuming the top job. Businesses have been added and long-term product lines have been sold, as Rometty reshapes the venerable firm into something aligned for today's target customers. Rometty's guiding principles throughout the migration? Don't protect the past; never be defined by your product; always transform yourself.[11] Given IBM's evolution from mechanical tabulators to mainframe computers, and manufacturing to consulting, information, cloud computing, and artificial intelligence, these principles could be a history lesson on the firm as much as Rometty's laws carrying them forward.

How would we describe the cultures of these firms? We will expand on culture in the final chapter of the book, but for now, recognize that culture is the outcome or manifestation of the behavior within the firm. I explain it that way as it is often simpler to describe a set of behaviors than a culture.

For me, innovative organizations exhibit these key behaviors and characteristics:

- Leadership is both paranoid and courageous. Paranoid, in that they appreciate and respect the market or industry dynamics, and know that some organization is always trying to take away their market, directly or indirectly. Courageous, as they are not afraid to move on from the safe waters of their current business model, service, or product line in a new direction.
- Employees are encouraged to experiment, test, challenge, and try new things. Just because we have always done something a particular way is often the best reason to challenge it, not to blindly accept it as is.
- The organization gets to know the boss. Customers are key, and these firms are hungry to know more about their customers, actively seeking to understand their needs, behaviors, goals, and habits more thoroughly.

- Recognizing that some of the best new or innovative ideas will come from other industries and markets, the firm exposes itself continually to outside influence and information.
- The organization understands that some ideas will fail. William McKnight, legendary chairman of 3M, knew that "the best and hardest work will be done in the spirit of adventure. Mistakes will be made."[12] The key is to capture the knowledge gained in those failures, refine and shape the ideas quickly, and carry on. The best strategies will have elements of new and unknown, things we have not done before, so failure will happen.
- There is a clearly identified champion for innovation within the leadership ranks of the firm. While this is often the CEO, it is not necessarily that individual. The executive champion for innovation pushes, challenges, asks tough questions, and ensures that the organization keeps an eye on tomorrow's customers while serving today's.

One may initially consider our theme of agility and find the connection to innovation obscure or abstract. It is important to appreciate the long-term perspective with leadership necessary in all organizations; innovation is critical for all of us, and an essential part of our strategy. Take the customer's perspective, and acknowledge that Lean and innovation together provide a path as simple as the reallocation of resources. This is where the innovation gap is the smallest and we can behave with agility.

ONE LAST STORY

In *Lean Innovation*,[13] I fearlessly predicted a number of changes in industry and society that would happen over the next decade. While that appendix to the main theme in the book was equal parts prediction, amusement, and rant, a few of the suggestions have come true or are evolving nicely. More homeowners are opting for cell phones only and not installing expensive landlines. We see fewer of the big, clunky desktop computers as more users opt for tablets and laptops. Fewer firms are asking us to "like them" on Facebook. Perhaps most interesting, doggie DNA testing has become a reality in some centers.*

---

* Before you say, "That stuff was obvious!" keep in mind the book was written in 2011 and early 2012.

Here is one that I got completely wrong—the number of wristwatch manufacturers will decline by 50%. Yep, I blew it. The leading indicator on this was behavioral within society. More millennials and young people (it makes me feel old just writing that phrase) use their phone to tell the time. The logical extension of that behavior is that fewer people will buy watches, and many watch companies would consolidate or go out of business.

While actual watch sales have declined,[14] I completely missed the advent of wearable technology, such as the Fitbit and Apple Watch. This whole category of connected devices has resulted in an explosion of new people wearing time-telling wrist-mounted devices, previously known as a watch. Because the devices also do a lot of other stuff—connect to the Internet, check your pulse, count your steps (why do you care?), and tell you when you received a text message—they are really not considered a watch, but are "wearable tech" and the next step in our creation of true cyborgs.

I have mixed feelings on this whole trend, loosely categorized as the *Internet of Things*. On the one hand, advocates believe the spread and implementation of such devices will result in orders of magnitude increases in productivity, as people will be blessed with not only all the available information they need to be contributing members of society, but also many of the mundane decisions and tasks, such as adjusting the thermostat, which will be done for us. Some of this makes sense. Sensors on a machine will be able to tell if a part is about to fail, order that part automatically through its Wi-Fi connection, and ask the firm's operating system to schedule maintenance to coincide with the arrival of that part. Your wearable tech device beeps when you have been sedentary too long (a feature known as "nagging"). Changing the oil on your vehicle now happens when the car tells you it needs to happen, rather than the old adage of doing it every 3000 miles or six months.

Keys, credit cards, and wallets are no longer required, as your phone will open your doors, turn on the lights, and pay for your food. Some people get geeked up about this type of thing (the early adopters), and I respect that. Every one of us is an early adopter with some element of society, and for these people, it is technology.

I remain somewhat skeptical, considering our history with certain technologies in society. Many of you will remember the days of VCRs, with their flashing clocks on the face because so few of us would reset the time after a power blip (discussed in Chapter 2), or those digital clocks in hotel rooms, with the time off by 10 minutes but we can't figure out how to reset them to the correct time. Consider again the Xbox example with my son at the start of the chapter—how long have computer and software companies been forcing updates on us and have yet to come up with a simpler process for it? Even the Apple Watch needs to be within connectivity range of an iPhone (which is often in your pocket); ultimately, why bother with the second piece of tech?* The implementation and advance of these technologies is dependent on our willingness to understand, connect, and then use the technology being offered us. Remember when people had mood rings and pet rocks? Remember when we actually wore devices that counted our steps?

All IoT products have three things in common: the base *physical* product that performs the function desired; the *smart* components, including sensors, storage, controls, or processors; and *connected* components to share, produce, or gather information appropriately.[15] Cost, therefore, will increase for the technology itself over its unconnected cousins. In the interest of productivity or efficiency gains within an organization's operations, the benefits could outweigh the initial cost, but implementation could be sluggish as advocates struggle with selling the concept, including the expense and training, to both skeptical leadership and unconvinced customers.

While the technology evolves and our cultural norms catch up, I offer a few ideas for developers of smart products and the IoT:

- The PubBit: Wearable tech that tracks the movement of your arm, to and from your mouth, with a mug of your favorite brew or dram of whiskey. The device will detect low beverage levels and auto-order according to user preferences. It includes a location override function that sends a signal indicating you are still at the office.
- The EmptyNest: A targeted thermostat that nudges hangers-on older offspring out the door by adjusting the temperature in their room warmer or cooler to uncomfortable temperatures. Works equally well with guests who have overstayed their welcome.
- Parental (or spousal) override on smart door locks: Miss the curfew and your smartphone will not open the door, but it will snap a picture with the onboard camera, posting the image to your social media account.

---

* Apple is reporting that sales of watches are off by 50% as of July 2016.

I like new things as much as the next person, especially if they are shiny or house more than 300 horsepower. While the above ideas are (somewhat) in jest, my overriding message to developers, investors, and adopters of wearable tech and the IoT products and services remains: *keep it simple.* Just because we can do something does not mean we should, despite the fact that someone might buy it. Does it offer value? Does it simplify things, eliminate the mundane, or free up time to focus on more important work? Is it easy to use and adaptable, and does it speak my language? When you can answer these questions in the affirmative, carry on. In the meantime, think about what you will do with all your free time when your world is automated.

REFERENCES

1. Burnton, S. 50 stunning Olympic moments No. 28: Dick Fosbury introduces 'the flop.' *The Guardian*, May 8, 2012.
2. Roberts, D. Marrying style with tech. *Fortune*, December 1, 2014, p. 30.
3. Olson, M., and Van Bever, D. *Stall Points—Most Companies Growing; Yours Doesn't Have to.* New Haven, CT: Yale University Press, 2008, p. 76.
4. Michel, S. Capture more value. *Harvard Business Review*, October 2014, pp. 79–80.
5. Kowitt, B. Fallen arches: Can McDonald's get its mojo back? *Fortune*, November 2014.
6. Soman, D. The innovator's challenge: Understanding the psychology of adoption. *Rotman Management Journal*, Fall 2014, pp. 5–7.
7. Tuerke, K., and Toman, S. Alien invasion. *University of Waterloo Alumni Magazine*, Spring 2015, p. 30.
8. Cross, B. *Lean Innovation: Understanding What's Next in Today's Economy.* Boca Raton, FL: CRC Press, 2012, p. 160.
9. *Managing Change and Transition.* Brighton, MA: Harvard Business School Press, 2003, p. 21.
10. Guglielmo, C. Where the glass is always half full. *Forbes*, September 23, 2013, pp. 90–92.
11. Lev-Ram, M. Getting past the big blues. *Fortune*, October 6, 2014, p. 94.
12. Birkenshaw, J., and Haas, M. Increase your return on failure. *Harvard Business Review*, May 2016, p. 90.
13. Cross, B. *Lean Innovation: Understanding What's Next in Today's Economy.* Boca Raton, FL: CRC Press, 2012, pp. 165–176.
14. Dilger, D.E. Swiss watch sales decline 2–3× faster than predicted as Apple Watch expands its reach. Apple Insider, October 20, 2015. http://appleinsider.com /articles/15/10/20/switch-watch-sales-decline-2-3x-faster-than-predicted-for -september-as-apple-watch-expands-its-reach.
15. Porter, M.E., and Heppelmann, J.E. How smart, connected products are transforming companies. *Harvard Business Review*, October 2015.

7

Communication and Selling the Plan

The single biggest problem with communication is the illusion it has taken place.

George Bernard Shaw

On December 11, 1998, NASA launched the Mars Climate Orbiter, a satellite roughly the size of a snowmobile and weighing 745 pounds. The Orbiter was part of a two-pronged, $193 million project (the other prong was a lander) to study the atmosphere, climate and climate change, and water conditions on the planet.

Unfortunately, on its first approach to Mars, 10 months later, the satellite passed too close to the planet and burned up in the Martian atmosphere. A review panel determined that the cause of the errant flight path was the result of trajectory information being transmitted to the Orbiter in English units rather than the metric units specified in the satellite's design. The difference in that information was enough to place the Orbiter too close to the planet's atmosphere, and the Orbiter was lost. Adding insult to injury, the Mars Polar Lander—the other half of the project—appeared to approach the planet at too high a velocity and crashed on December 3, 1999. Neither vehicle was able to transmit any information, and the mission was a failure.

What we had here was a failure to communicate.

Having trajectory signals transmitted in metric seems like a simple enough process, but in sending English units rather than metric, the two systems were effectively speaking different languages. This is not a new or even uncommon phenomenon. We have all had situations where our intent was lost in the translation, and the receiving party misinterprets our message. More often than not, this is our fault, not theirs, as our ability to communicate effectively is not as well developed as we would like to think. Translation and calculation errors are one challenge, often having significant or even disastrous impacts on a project or initiative, as noted above.*

More germane to the focus of this book, think about the strategies and plans developed by organizations everywhere. The leadership team has wrapped up the planning process, having spent weeks and many person-hours understanding customer needs and the evolution of the market, and allocating resources to position the firm successfully over the next year. As one of those executives, you would like to say that you then communicate the plan effectively to your team, enabling your team to then carry out the plan and bring that strategy to fruition, creating value internally and for your customers. Everyone is excited. During the subsequent year in question, you follow up with the team on a regular basis, ensuring the plan is going well and everyone has the resources they need. Questions are answered, roadblocks are eliminated, and we approach the end of the year having hit all objectives, building customer enthusiasm and employee morale to new levels.

Or, perhaps not. Management in most industries and businesses is notorious for leaving out those last steps, the communication and management of the plan. We may do the town hall meetings, mapping out what the new strategy is, but the statistics indicate that the people on the receiving end of the message—that is, the people with the responsibility to execute the plan—really do not understand the plan itself and, worse, are unable in most cases to connect their work to the plan. People cannot do what they do not understand. Many studies support these statements, but here are a few of the statistics, from a 2002 Watson Wyatt study of 12,000 U.S. workers published by FranklinCovey:[†]

- Just 15% of employees were able to identify the organization's goals and priorities.
- 51% of employees did not understand what they were supposed to do in their roles to accomplish organizational goals or priorities.
- Only 3% believe there is a line of sight between their work and company objectives, while 27% believe there is no connection between their work and company objectives.

---

[*] Christopher Columbus even struggled with unit calculations, when he apparently used Roman miles in calculating Earth's circumference, rather than nautical miles, which led to him ultimately thinking he had arrived in Asia rather than the Caribbean in 1492.

[†] See The execution quotient: The measure of what matters. Cambridge, ON: FranklinCovey, 2003. http://www.franklincovey.ca/FCCAWeb/mmedia/pdf/library/xQWhitePaper.pdf.

- Only 19% of employees feel passionate about company goals.
- Employees spend only 49% of their time on company priorities.
- Only 19% of employees believe their organization actively removes barriers to achieving company goals.
- Only 23% of employees believe there is accountability for the goals and objectives established by the firm.

These numbers can be disheartening for any of us, and as a result, we often remain skeptical of such data. Monitor Consulting, Bain Consulting, McKinsey, and others have and continue to study what I refer to as *alignment* on an ongoing basis, however, and we are really not improving. Alignment is the cornerstone of the A³ model discussed earlier, and without it, an organization cannot achieve either appreciation of roles or assurance of completion of the firm's plan. That is, any progress we make is happenstance, resulting in an ongoing difference in the performance of the organization versus its initial plan. We underperform, creating what I call the execution gap (Figure 7.1).

The good news is that like a lot of what we have discussed in this book, the solution is simple (but naturally, not easy). Despite our struggles, people do communicate. We developed the ability to speak shortly after we discovered fire ("Watch out! That's hot!"), and while we have not progressed as far as would have been ideal over the millennia since, with

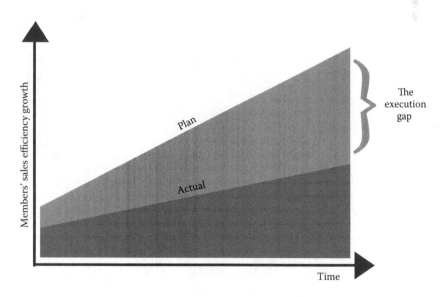

FIGURE 7.1
Execution gap.

appropriate attention, we can figure this out. We, as leadership, can sell the plan to our associates, communicate priorities, and connect their work to those initiatives. We can build in follow-up mechanisms to ensure we are progressing with the plan through the year, holding each other account-able and celebrating the victories. This is not new.

The final component of the agility cycle (Figure 7.2) is communication, and we will sort through an effective approach in this chapter that will enable an organization to bring the plan, and its strategy, to life. We will look at communication necessary to sell the plan, the follow-up associated with managing the plan, and even then, the ongoing communication we would apply to reinforce the plan, and in fact begin to shift the culture of the firm toward one of execution.

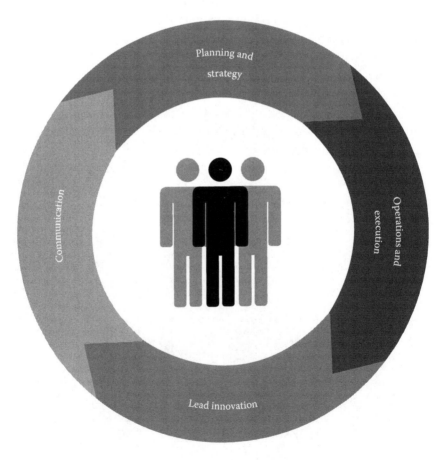

FIGURE 7.2
Agility cycle.

This is part of our role as leadership; we own it. Change and strategy create a shift in our goals and priorities, resulting in new objectives and "work" for our teams. That change leads to tension, and leaders must manage that tension and ensure alignment and clarity of purpose.[1]

SELLING THE PLAN: THE INITIAL COMMUNICATION

In Chapter 5, I suggested that an appropriate target in the development of an operating plan is to have it complete two months prior to the start of the next fiscal year. "Complete," in this case, means in the terminal interpretation of the word; everything is done—financials approved, project leads assigned, gaps eliminated, and the organization is ready to move on the key elements of the plan. Essentially, there are no loose ends. That two-month window is your time to sell the plan to the people who will do the work. Think of the statistics presented earlier—this is where you bring your organization's numbers up closer to 100% understanding, alignment, appreciation, and assurance.

How do you do this in your firm? Single-site entities can manage this process easily and quickly. Shut down operations where possible, or plan multiple events when operations cannot be halted. Allocate an hour, but plan to only talk for 20 or 30 minutes. Some other guidelines are

- Think SCR—simple, clear, and repeatable with key themes: customer focus, elimination of bottlenecks, less waste, speaking now, and so forth.
- Tell stories. Connect your message and theme to events in industry, customer anecdotes, and employee situations. Stories connect and make it memorable for employees. Your stories will often become their stories.
- Use microphones. Not everyone hears well,* and the acoustics in many rooms that hold dozens of people may be poor.

---

* I had my hearing checked a couple years ago, partly due to a bit of ringing (tinnitus), and Katrina indicating she didn't think I was listening. The ear-nose-throat specialist did a comprehensive battery of tests and indicated all was good, other than a partial loss in the 4000 Hz range. "OK," I said, "what is in that range?" "That, my friend, is the range most women with softer voices speak in." I smiled. That diagnosis has since come up a number of times around the house. *Priceless.*

- Allow time for questions and clarification, especially when this plan may be different than what you brought out a year ago.
- Anticipate the skeptics. My colleagues Peter Richardson and Elspeth Murray use the ratio 70/20/10, where 70% of your population will generally be on board, 20% will actively endorse and help drive the plan, and 10% will just as actively push back. Plan to meet with this group separately to get them on board, although you may never get to 100% buy-in. Anyone actively detracting from the plan will get a chance to come around, or you may have to move them to positions of less influence or even remove them from the firm.
- Keep the language simple and understandable by all. This is not the place to demonstrate your command of language and vocabulary if it means people do not understand the message or theme of the plan.

Bill Belichick, longtime coach of the New England Patriots in the NFL, is a master of obfuscation in his communication, especially in media interviews. That is, he can talk and make the media feel like they are getting something without really saying anything. Here is an example:

> Then we talked about it and thought about ways maybe to put some pressure on the defense with that concept of having more receivers on the field than were actually eligible. To make them ineligible instead of making an ineligible guy eligible, to go the other way around. We came up with a few ideas.[2]

What? OK, Belichick is doing this on purpose, but it is a great example. Your operating plan rollout is not the time for this sort of ambiguity or lack of clarity in a message. Think *simple, clear,* and *repeatable.* Change guru Harvard's John Kotter believes that if you can't communicate a vision to someone in five minutes or less, and get a reaction that signifies both understanding and interest, you are not communicating the plan effectively.[3] The strategy roadmap is often a good tool here and useful in these presentations.

Keep in mind that the onus is on us as leadership to communicate our vision in a manner people understand and appreciate; it is not up to those on the receiving end of the message to figure out what we are saying. Taking the time to prepare and deliver a message clearly is a fundamental part of our execution process. The moment they understand the goals and vision of the organization, we are already in a better position than those firms highlighted in FranklinCovey's statistics that kicked off the chapter. Look at it this way:

- Employees who understand the message are better able to connect their work to the firm's strategy.
- If a team member can relate his or her responsibilities back to the vision and direction of the firm, we generally see a higher sense of buy-in to both organizational objectives and the team member's own work. Diligence and quality of work increase.
- Work that does not connect to a strategy (i.e., work that does not add value or support customer need) is more likely to be challenged, potentially freeing up resources by eliminating non-value-added work we would have otherwise kept doing.
- Creativity is enhanced, as the direction of the organization is now always in the back of employees' minds. Opportunities are identified, discussed, and pursued where possible.
- Even suppliers appreciate increased involvement and inclusion in our plan. When they understand our direction and feel part of that strategy, they are more often likely to share new ideas and commit to keeping projects and commitments intact.

REINFORCING THE PLAN: FOLLOWING UP

Many executives and managers have initiated new programs or kicked off a campaign with some type of town hall meeting. Sadly, fewer of these executives demonstrate true leadership with their teams and follow up to solidify the potential for a plan to come to fruition. Without a comprehensive approach to keep the plan moving over the course of the year, many such initiatives, however important, strategic, or "game changing," die a quiet and anonymous death.

Strategic plans usually include new and uncertain elements, which result in additional work or effort for many within our workforce. New leadership especially will face skepticism and reluctance in a larger part of the employee base, as many adopt a "wait and see" or "this too shall pass" mindset. The first few months of a new plan are the most important; this is where you as a leadership team get past the inertia of past experience

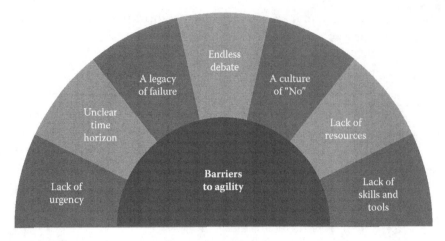

FIGURE 7.3
Barriers to agility.

within the business, or you flame out. Figure 7.3 highlights some of the behavioral and cultural obstacles you will face in driving a new plan forward. The elements in the diagram will all be familiar, with a key message that the path of least resistance is not your best course in the execution of your plan. Communicating, securing buy-in, and delivering the plan is not something we can leave to chance; we have to work at it.

Follow-up is essential to the plan's execution, and while I am no fan of creating extra meetings on your schedule, an effective operating plan meeting is one that will pay huge dividends for the organization. You will develop a structure and format for your own meeting, but consider these elements in your approach:

- Cross-functional participation, with both the owners or sponsors of key initiatives for the coming year, and leadership representatives from other departments in the organization supporting those projects.
- Attendees should bring their copies of the operating plan, review notes they made at the prior meetings, and collectively approach all deliverables with a goal of progress and closure.
- Sponsors may bring key project people with them to the meeting to debrief on key project elements. Note that this meeting in no way replaces any of the meetings normally associated with particular projects.

- Focus on the tactics and projects in the plan that were created to deliver the firm's strategy. This is not a meeting where the leadership team reviews or spends time rehashing vision and direction; table that dialogue for the annual planning process.
- Hold the meeting monthly while the organization makes solid progress on the plan. If an initiative begins to slide, commit additional time to that initiative itself; don't burden the whole operating plan process with additional meetings on specific plan elements that require additional attention.

One can see that with the approach to the meeting and who is in attendance, the organization is essentially formalizing a process to follow up on company goals and objectives. This maintains leadership engagement in the process and illustrates to the rest of the firm that the organization remains committed to the vision communicated at the end of the previous year. For executives and sponsors to talk about an initiative in front of their peers like this, by default, they will have to be up to speed on the progress of that project. This leads to more informal discussions and involvement in the organization's operations, and the rest of the employee base will see that involvement as commitment to the plan. As the saying goes, great leaders are where the action is. The operating plan meeting may feel like we are managing a process or following a script, but what we are really doing is managing people. Former Milwaukee Bucks owner Jim Fitzgerald used to say, "When you get involved with business, you only have two problems: People and Money."[4] The operating plan meeting is about managing your people and, as an outcome, taking an active role in managing the execution of your strategy.

GOOD AND BAD COMMUNICATION

Please be aware that if your spoken words include personal or sensitive information, that information will be among the data captured and transmitted to a third party through our use of voice recognition.[5]

How do you feel about that statement? It is certainly a bit spooky, and perhaps Orwellian. The statement itself is considered "industry standard," however, by firms such as Samsung, and is included in many of the terms of use most of us just agree to and move on. Without batteries of lawyers and some sort of all-out consumer rebellion, those terms of use and phrases like this have likely become industry standard by default. Companies implemented the language, we clicked *Accept*, and a law was effectively passed. In hindsight, our agreement to these terms is an indication that we were not really listening. While we have not had to really pay for that oversight yet, I expect the time will come when we regret that habit of premature or apathetic acceptance.

Effective communication, then, has three components: a message, a sender or speaker, and a receiver or listener. We have discussed the message component—the content of both the plan and your process for rolling out the plan. The speaker is you or another member of the leadership team. The missing component to the dialogue within this chapter, then, is a more detailed appreciation of the people on the receiving end of the message—your employees, suppliers, board members, family and friends, and especially customers. How you position and design your message will have a significant impact on not only what people hear, but also how they interpret your intent and meaning.

The aforementioned terms of use example aside, most of our organizations would not obfuscate an important message in a manner that people will naturally ignore, at least not intentionally. Yet that is the outcome of so many of our communication strategies—that many of our listening audience are growing weary and simply ignoring us; for example,

- A major business magazine I subscribed to (note the past tense) began sending me renewal notices *one month* into a yearlong subscription. While this one was clearly over the top, most of us have grown so numb to the too frequent reminders of pending expiration that we wait until they are at the point of suspending service before renewing. Not only is this tedious, but it is a waste of resources.
- Despite a growing ability through analytics and experience to really identify target customers and markets, few companies consider those customers in much of their branding and marketing activities. Television ads during the Super Bowl, for example, run several million dollars for a 30-second spot. The ad may be viewed by millions of people, but how many of those people really care about the product or service being advertised? The answer is, most don't; brand recognition goes up, but the majority of these people are not buyers.

- The engineering and technical community is notorious for the application of three-letter acronyms (which they humorously dub TLAs) and other technical terms. Most of those are fine within their domain, but customers, executives, and other team members need the benefit of comprehension. A colleague at Autosystems, an automotive parts company I was with for a number of years, was debugging a technical issue we had with our coating systems in one of the facilities. He and his team eventually came up with a solution to the issue. I asked him what they did. He said, "Well, we put in a surfactant, and that seemed to eliminate the problem." I looked around the room—some people were nodding sagely, "Ah yes, a surfactant! Thank goodness Scott is on our team!" Others were clearly confused. So I said, "A surfactant, you say. You mean you dumped in some soap?" He turned a bit red, paused, and said, "Well, it's a bit more complicated than that, but yes, we added a detergent."*

The tongue is the stupidest muscle in your body, and has been proven to disable hearing when it is engaged, but when you exercise it properly, it can have a magical effect on the ears of people nearby. Yogi Berra, former baseball player and coach, was among the best at this; every time he spoke, he made you think. "You can observe a lot just by watching" and "If you don't set goals, you can't regret not reaching them" are a couple of his quotations that are appropriate even in our context here.

Few of us are as creative or perhaps wired the way Yogi was, but if we keep a few simple things in mind, the message may reach its destination.

- Person-to-person is always best; phones are a close second. Email is not communicating (see Appendix A for more on email). Email may be a means to transfer information, but you have little ability to assess comprehension, tone, intent, and interest if you cannot look someone in the eye.
- My friend Don Warren reminds me that you can say almost anything with a smile on your face. Keep that in mind with your next tough discussion.

---

* There were a handful of times over the years that I could call on the learnings of my undergraduate degree in biology and chemistry, and this was one. I recalled the discussion in organic chemistry about surfactants (surface-active agents), which include detergents and other emulsifiers. Not the same as a soap, but I got his attention.

- When it comes to a presentation, start with a story and end with a story. Stories can provide context, hook an audience, and endear them to the speaker. We all like to be entertained, so this is one of those *life skills*.
- Silence can be just as effective as speaking in your communication toolkit. I think women figured this one out a long time ago. Beware especially the silence that follows a "hmph."
- When in doubt, remember the first bullet. In fact, Toyota built this into its Toyota Production System as Principle 12: *go and see*. Go talk to someone, have a coffee, and make sure you are all on the same page.

The last link in the agility cycle connects our work to the vision and objectives of the firm. Without this connection, we are wasting our time and scarce organizational resources. The single biggest reason a plan fails is a lack of comprehension and buy-in from the people responsible for its execution. Therefore, take the time and tell your story.

ONE LAST STORY

Our family was in the Caribbean on vacation in the spring of 2015, and the resort we were at offered an evening boat cruise with some snacks and cocktails and a chance to watch the sunset over the bay. The boat was about 40 feet long, and there were about 20 guests on the deck as we cruised along.

About halfway into the tour, the captain changed course and we sped up, moving quickly over to where there was a man in the water splashing around. Seventy-five yards away was the Hobie Cat small sailboat he had signed out from his resort, floating idly with his wife or girlfriend waving for help. Maritime law necessitated our detour to assist the couple, but that was just the start of the story.

We approached the man first, as he was obviously not supported by a boat or floatation device of any kind. As we neared, he called up to us:

Man: Do you have a scuba mask?
Captain: What?
Man: Do you have a scuba mask? I dropped my GoPro camera in the water.

Captain: Sir, are you in any distress at all? Are you OK?

Man: I'm OK. Just need to find the camera. It sunk when it fell off the boat.

Captain: Sir, is that your Hobie Cat over there? It seems to be floating away.

Man: Yes, that's us. My girlfriend doesn't know how to sail.

The captain paused.

This guy is floating in the water about 15 feet from us. Any number of us could have jumped in and helped if he looked like he was in trouble, or we could have thrown him a line and pulled him to the rear of the boat. At this point, however, having heard the exchange, the guests all started looking around. Is this part of the entertainment? Does the crew have a camera pointed at us? Nope—this was a genuine situation.

Think for a minute here—what is your impression of the man based on this communication? Clearly, he was not thinking, you might say, having abandoned his girlfriend who doesn't sail for a $400 camera. Her sailboat, by the way, is drifting out to sea, far faster than he could ever swim to catch up to it. When she is recovered, this will be ugly, and we would all foretell a very short relationship.

The problem is, our assumption of the man is based on only half the story, a problem we have all experienced. We make assumptions based on incomplete information, often before a message has been completely communicated. This was indeed the situation here as well.

Captain: Your girlfriend, in that boat over there that is drifting out to sea, doesn't sail?

Man: Yes. So, do you have a scuba mask on board? I'll be able to see the camera better with a mask.

Captain: OK sir, here is what we are going to do. We will pull you on board now, and then head over to your girlfriend and put you both on the sailboat. Why did you take off your life jacket, by the way? Everyone on a Hobie Cat has to have a life jacket on.

Man: I couldn't dive below the surface with the jacket on. How else would I pick up the camera?

Although we are still only getting half the picture, most people on the boat are admittedly forming a fairly clear opinion of the man by now. Most people are smiling; the man was in no danger with our boat and crew floating nearby (unless we consider the danger from his girlfriend), and the boat would easily reach the woman floating away once we retrieved the man and steamed in her direction. One couple on the deck near me articulated an opinion that this was a charade and part of our entertainment that afternoon, reaffirming my earlier thought.

Although the man was adamant about sticking with his task and retrieving his GoPro camera, the captain had the final say in the matter and one of the deck hands helped him board the ladder onto the back of the boat. We were soon underway to reunite the man with his girlfriend. When we neared their Hobie Cat sailboat, she called out, "Did you get it?"

Man: No, I couldn't see anything down there.
Woman: Damn it! I just paid $400 for that thing. Well, get on and we can go back and look some more.

Instantly, our opinions changed. We had new information, details previously not available but now key in clarifying the picture. Our new conclusion was that the woman sent the man into the water to risk life and limb in retrieving the camera. Several other conclusions could be inferred at the same time:

- The couple had not been dating very long, certainly no more than a year or two at the longest. There comes a time in a relationship where the man would respond in the negative to the suggestion that he dives in after a camera, while his wife or girlfriend, who is unable to pilot the sailboat by herself, drifts out to sea. Looking downward over the side of the boat, he might say, "Yeah, I don't think so. That's a damn shame." Eventually, the logic muscle overrides the gallant hero muscle. They would squabble or perhaps even laugh about it, and buy another in the duty-free store on the way home.
- These two are meant for each other.

The man was helped back onto his boat, which we offered to tow to the shore (I think to minimize any liability should the couple pursue their GoPro salvage efforts), but they declined. The captain radioed their resort to keep an eye on them, and with a stern warning to forget about the camera, we headed back to our resort and never saw the couple again.

The purpose of the story here is to highlight the risk associated with your audience getting insufficient information to understand and appreciate the full picture associated with your vision and strategy. People are smart and intuitive, and nature abhors a vacuum. In the absence of a full and complete picture, your employees will naturally fill in the blanks based on previous talks, their experience, or the comments of others around them. With something as important as the strategic plan, leadership simply cannot afford people having to interpret the message—they need to be thorough, clear, and patient while going over the vision numerous times in numerous ways.

Consider, finally, the application of other media in communicating the plan, but do so with caution. Signs, websites, videos, and other media are one way—people reading them cannot, in most cases, ask questions, so they may be drawing their own conclusions again. Look at Figure 7.4 as an example.

This sign hangs in the local sports dome where my son and I play some tennis over the winter. I had seen the sign a dozen times when I eventually

FIGURE 7.4
Moira Vet Clinic.

FIGURE 7.5
No Wi-Fi.

realized I was interpreting its message incorrectly. Recall the scotoma discussion from earlier in the book—my mind had made a decision regarding what the sign was about without involving me in any reasonable thought process. Perhaps it was the bold title. I had glanced at the sign and thought, "Hey, great, we have a clinic nearby for veterans." In my defense, there is a military base close by, and therefore a large retired military population. They deserve their own clinic. Sadly, no. This one was obviously for pets and animals, and I am sure they do a good job. Yet again, the incorrect interpretation of a message, and dummies like me arrive at the wrong conclusion.

This last one is just for fun, and a sign of the times (Figure 7.5). It was seen outside a restaurant in Penn Station, Manhattan, in March 2016. Worth a thought.

REFERENCES

1. Edmonson, A. Wicked problem solvers. *Harvard Business Review*, June 2016, p. 54.
2. Maaddi, R. Belichick puts a new wrinkle on an old concept. *Globe and Mail*, January 16, 2015.
3. Kotter, J. Leading change: Why transformation efforts fail. *Harvard Business Review*, January 2007.
4. Lawrence, A. Franchise player. *Fortune*, July 21, 2014, p. 18.
5. Westhoven, J. Your television may be spying on you. CNN HLN, February 9, 2015. http://www.cnn.com/videos/tech/2015/02/09/samsung-eavesdropping-tv.hln.

8

Agile Culture

If I am cold, I will build a fire or stamp my feet.
I won't ask you for a blanket.

Two of the classic works in science fiction literature are the *Robot* and *Foundation* collections by sci-fi master Isaac Asimov, which map the relationship between humans, robots, and society over a period of 10,000 years (starting when Susan Calvin begins work with US Robots in 2007). At a defining point in the series, around the year 3700, a sentient robot by the name of Giskard makes the decision to permit the villain to activate a device that renders Earth uninhabitable, forcing humanity to evacuate the planet and take to the stars well ahead of "schedule."[1] Giskard's logic was that the survival and evolution of our species would depend on us moving far more quickly and essentially out of our comfort zones. Giskard made it impossible to stay on Earth.

Logic such as this is not unlike the idea of settlers burning their ships when they arrive at the "new world," forcing themselves to find a way to survive and not return home.

What if we applied that same logic to our own lives? Could the potential of a long life (80+ years) discourage risk or innovation? At some point, do we "relax" a bit, and perhaps put things on cruise control? Are we still taking risks in our forties, fifties, and sixties with new ideas, products, services, or business lines, or are we making the existing elements of our careers and lives work? When was the last time you truly stepped outside your comfort zone with an innovation, new career, or personal pursuit?

How much more innovative would society be if we all died at the age of 40? That is, if the maximum age of our species was four decades, when everything was genetically programmed to "shut down," would that make us more or less aggressive with making the most of that time?

Let's take the same perspective with our corporations. I have asked this of you before: If your organization ceased to exist tomorrow, would anyone notice? For many organizations, the truth is a bit more bleak than they acknowledge. We are seeing the extinction of retail giants, technology companies, logistics providers, airlines, manufacturers, hoteliers, and restaurant chains at an increasing pace. Whereas the average tenure of a firm on the Standard and Poor's 500 was 67 years in 1920, firms disappear from the list in 15 years today. By 2027, it is estimated that 75% of firms on the list now will be replaced.* That is, three in four of our organizations risk being sold, shut down, or marginalized within 10 years. Other like-minded research suggests that one in three public firms will not survive the next five years.[2]

The appropriate follow-up question, then, is, *unless we do what*? Even in firms that are currently "healthy," the data suggests the shine may be dimming. Profits and revenues were down 4.2% in Fortune 500 companies in 2015, yet employment at these same firms increased and productivity declined.[3]

Recall our initial discussion early in the first chapter of the book: Why are we here? Why is our organization in business? The answer is certainly not about being mediocre, an also-ran, or a firm just taking up a chair at the business table; we are here to create value and excel in our particular area of focus. The organization was built to solve a problem or fill a need, regardless of its industry.

Here is another look at our life cycle curve, henceforth to be referred to as our business model life cycle (Figure 8.1). Consider your own organization. Where would you be positioned on this curve? Could you prove it?

Sadly, it is far too common a situation where our leadership has an overconfident, often introverted perspective of our firm's position on the life cycle. Many of these firms believe they are still climbing the curve, interpreting short-term or false growth as continued success, where others believe the plateau they are on is a result of "temporary" economic conditions or other external factors. The reality is, if you are not growing, you are slowing and being passed by. When was the last time you did something *new*?

If you really believe the firm is growing, you can likely prove it, with data, numbers, and analytics. These should be your sounding board and

---

* For the work of Yale lecturer Richard Foster, see Lam, B. Where do firms go when they die? *The Atlantic*, April 12, 2015. http://www.theatlantic.com/business/archive/2015/04/where-do-firms-go-when-they-die/390249/.

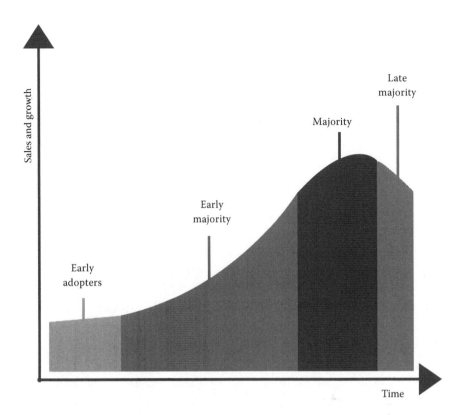

FIGURE 8.1
Business model life cycle.

reality check. While that "reality" shifts every time we tell a story or remember an event, data is pure and meaningful. What is yours telling you? Firms that exhibit exploratory behavior consider and react to customer needs, create their own opportunities, and drive their next business cycle. Leadership that permits economic conditions and other events to dictate their situation allow business cycles to happen to them.

Consider the culture in your organization. How would you describe it?

- Are employees proud to work with the firm? Is it just a job (which may be fine)? Are people actively looking for other opportunities?
- Are employees truly empowered?* Will they ask questions, bring ideas and solutions to discussions, and solve problems as they arise?

---

* However cliché the word *empowerment* is in today's business world, when applied correctly, it remains the most effective description of employees who believe in their ability to make an impact at all levels of their operations.

- Do you, as a leader, balance your time between supporting team members, direct reports, and company initiatives, and executing your own responsibilities and planning for what may be next for the organization?
- Would insiders use words like *inclusive, decisive, responsive, involved,* or *agile* when describing the organization, or would you hear words like *bureaucratic, sluggish,* or *introverted*?

In the 1990s, one of the most successful and fastest-growing firms in Canada was a company called Nortel Networks (formerly Northern Telecom, and Northern Electric). Nortel was known for its phone systems provided to commercial and corporate facilities, but really had a strong foundation in switches and the supporting electronic architecture that was the backbone and brains of enterprise communication systems. Nortel's stock grew consistently for a number of years, and the company was a place people were proud to work for. Indeed, when you met a Nortel employee at a social event or other gathering and asked them what they did, the response was more often than not, "I work for Nortel."

Fast-forward 10 years, and the company is in decline. Nortel is on its fourth CEO in four years, funds have been mismanaged, sales are declining, and past executives are being investigated. Nortel filed for protection from creditors in 2009, and was eventually purchased by American telecommunications giant Avaya (formerly Lucent) later that year. Avaya brought it back from the brink of extinction, although what were Nortel's operations remain a shadow of their former dominance in the market, having been swallowed up by a competitor.

Ask those same employees now what they do for a living, and a more common response is "I am an engineer or programmer." These are still talented, highly capable individuals doing good work and passionate about their field, but in many cases, the subtle belief or perception is that the company abandoned them, and forgot about the people who made them great in the 1980s and 1990s.

Compare Nortel with firms like Southwest Airlines, Four Seasons Hotels, Zappos, or Apple—firms that excel in their particular landscape by almost all measures—and you could easily draw a parallel between an effective culture and the performance of the company. In short, people who enjoy their work and the people they work with outperform those that do not. Booz and Company studied a number of firms and found the impact of the organization's culture on performance is profound, concluding that even with the right strategy, a sluggish or misaligned culture could doom that strategy. In their words, culture trumps strategy every time.[4]

Where does our culture come from? We talk about or even blame our culture for all that is wrong, often without considering what culture is. Simply put, our culture comes from leadership, and is made up of the collective behavior around the firm. That collective behavior is a result of how we interpret the behavior of leadership, how we are compensated, how we work and play, and how people solve problems or respond to our customers. A question I like to ask executives and students is, if you had the culture you wanted, what would the behavior look like around the organization? Would those behaviors align with the strategy and direction? Could you provide examples of behavior now that represent your culture?

Here is a short case, a simple, single-project-level example, but consider the following teleconference for the regional operations of a courier service and the culture within the firm:

> Every Monday at 3 p.m., the regional director "meets" with his controller and six of his direct reports for a conference call. The direct reports are each responsible for one of the municipal sorting centers in that region. The purpose of the call is for a quick business update from the director to his team, and for each manager to report out on progress against short-term goals in his or her area of responsibility. The calls normally run 30–45 minutes.

You are the director.

You: OK. Everyone is on the call now, so we'll get started. I have two updates from head office [*director delivers updates*]. Any questions? Good. Let's go "around the room." Kingston, why don't you start?

Kingston: Actually, we had a good week. We are focusing on absenteeism and sorting equipment uptime as KOIs* right now. Absenteeism was down a half percent to 2.6% last week. Machine uptime was up 3%–86% from Wednesday on. We did a PM on Tuesday, which was a month ahead of schedule, and that made a big difference. We'll be adjusting our PM schedule from twice to three times per year on that process as a result.

You: What did you do to reduce absenteeism?

---

* KOI, key operating indicator; PM, preventative maintenance; Kaizen, an approach to continuous improvement and Lean methodology.

Kingston: Well, nothing fancy, really. We had our monthly employee meeting a week ago Friday. I showed our performance next to the rest of the divisions and talked about why we track this metric. No one wants to be Kaizened out of a job, so they're getting behind it.

You: Sounds effective. What about the Lean project going on in your receiving area?

Kingston: On track. We expect to wrap up next week. The savings look pretty much as we mapped out.

You: Great work, Kingston. OK, Pembroke?*

Pembroke: Hi everyone. We didn't fare so well this week. We are tracking package mutilation as a KOI and it's gone up the last three weeks in a row. We're at 1.3% now, and can't seem to make any headway on this. We also lost the project manager for the plant reorganization initiative last week. She is the third person we've lost to UPS in a couple of months. These resource issues are starting to really bog us down.

You: [How do you respond?]

How would you react in this situation with the circumstances as presented by the Pembroke manager, and with the Pembroke manager himself? There seems to be a stark difference in both approach and performance between the Pembroke site and Kingston. On the one hand, Kingston is dialed in (and not just for the conference call), action-oriented, and solving problems. On the other hand, Pembroke appears to be over his head, unsure of the cause of the problems, and losing team members to the competition. We could say that there is a problem with that individual in Pembroke, but it is also likely there is a broader cultural issue within that facility. People are waiting for things to happen, help to arrive, or for a change in leadership and the next "new plan."

As I indicated, this is a fairly simple example, and after appropriate investigation, most of us would provide assistance if this is a new manager in Pembroke, or replace him if the individual has been around for a while. In a larger sense, however, how would you approach the situation if it appeared the culture in Pembroke was not aligned to your strategy, or lacking any real inclination toward execution?

---

* Just for fun, try reading the character of Pembroke in the case with the voice of Eeyore from *Winnie-the-Pooh*™.

Have you, or others in your organization, ever tried to change the culture of the firm? Often compared with turning an ocean liner at sea, changing our culture is a slow, often tenuous and fragile course of action that requires continuous focus and attention on our part as leadership. If culture is the manifestation of our collective behavior within the firm, changing culture should really be as simple as modifying our behavior.

Perhaps not *simple*, but adjusting individual and collective behavior is our last step in building true organizational agility, and in fact need not be the elephant in the room we are often afraid to tackle (Figure 8.2). Culture has garnered a lot of attention over the years in business research and publication. In fact, the field of organizational behavior spends a significant portion of its time and focus on the idea of understanding and improving

FIGURE 8.2
Agility cycle.

culture. While the field has been published and discussed widely, sluggish or restrictive culture remains a significant barrier against getting things done and realizing agility. I do not think this is a result of a lack of good ideas or not understanding how to fix the problem; I believe the issue is a lack of appreciation within many leadership groups of the impact their culture has on performance, and the amount of work and commitment it will take to turn the ocean liner and point it in the right direction.

I will not try to summarize the collective research on changing culture here, but I will discuss it in the context of the book and hopefully give you a few ideas on achieving an agile culture. I will start with another look at the barriers to agility we discussed earlier in the book (Figure 8.3).

When we examine the barriers to driving change and strategy within the firm, we may note that several of those same barriers would slow down or obstruct our efforts to improve culture. If leadership or members of the organization do not perceive the connection between effective culture and organizational success, there exists a lack of urgency.

Think of your own attempts to change or improve something in your life, perhaps to eat better, exercise more, or quit smoking, and how difficult it is to really make that change stick. Our behaviors are exactly that—an ongoing series of acts, entrenched ways of doing things, built into us in a form of muscle or psychological memory. This is the way we are programmed, and we are trying to rewrite the code while the system is operating. In the absence of continuous support, coaching, and prioritization, we revert to previously accepted behavior, resulting in another failed attempt (a legacy

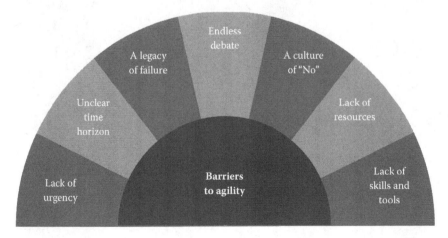

FIGURE 8.3
Barriers to agility.

of failure). Even if this is the first serious attempt at culture change within the firm, and we have properly set the table with incentives, follow-up, and an appreciation of why it needs to happen now, as leaders we have to recognize how easy it is for employees to revert to past behavior.

In appreciation of the fact that all our organizations are different, and your needs will vary from the specific needs of another reader, I present the next section in what I refer to as a *culture buffet*. It includes and outlines a number of excellent approaches to changing and modifying culture and behavior within the firm that have been proven either through my own experience or in documented situations within various areas of industry. Pick two or three that make the most sense to you, that fit either your situation or the specific needs of your operations, and carry on. Circle back to the buffet when the need arises.

IMPROVING CULTURE

Connect Culture to Strategy

Focus on behavior in the organization that will have an impact on the firm's strategy. If, for example, you have expressed a mandate for improving customer service, an essential component will be faster response among frontline employees. In this case, you would emphasize the idea of solving a customer's problem on the first phone call or interaction, and provide the training and resources to make that possible. You might then implement a key operating indicator that measured the number of customer challenges that were resolved on the first interaction, and publish and follow up on that metric.* Before long, employees are doing the stuff we measure and talk about.

Reflect on Best Practices

Many firms use the term *best practice* to describe the most appropriate approach in dealing with a particular situation, be it an engineering solution or other form of standardization, often in the interest of not repeating a past problem or failure witnessed by the organization. My own

---

* Keep in mind that we often track a metric far longer than is appropriate. A metric should only be in place as long as it is measuring something important. After the situation has been resolved or corrected, consider replacing that metric with the next challenge.

experience in this area is that a best practice has a shelf life; it was a very appropriate solution at the time, but our operations change so quickly that we should not blindly accept the statement "That is our best practice" and move on.* John Kotter of Harvard University suggests asking whether best practices still apply, as they often produce less satisfying results today than when first derived.[5]

Are We Asking the Right Questions?

I have said before that good leaders ask good questions. We don't always have the answers, but we need to be able to ask questions that lead the team in the direction of a solution. Sometimes those questions are difficult, forcing discussion or consideration in areas we may not be comfortable, but an effective culture will support such questions. Consider these examples:

- Are our customers loyal due to our processes or switching costs, or as a result of good service?
- If donors had to choose between two charitable causes, would they support our not-for-profit?
- Would the government fund our branch or agency if it was not already in existence? That is, would we receive funding and endorsement as a new entity?
- Would a CEO or other executive read our research with interest, or are we targeting other researchers?
- Could our policies prevent the right behavior, or promote inappropriate behavior?

There was a situation at an airport in British Columbia in 2015, where a man was forced to miss a flight as a result of an inappropriate policy. He had an artificial hip, which "always beeps" when passing through the metal detector in security. Many smaller airports have yet to install the full-body scanners, relying on frisking and patting down passengers when necessary. In this case, there were only female security officers on duty, and they cited the "same-sex" policy and refused to pat the gentleman down. As a result, he missed his flight to a family wedding in Ontario, and

---

* It is fair to say that some best practices may never go out of style. Think airport security—having more eyes (human or electronic) on the crowd still seems appropriate.

had to pay a $100 change fee on his flight as a result of the situation. The Canadian Air Transport Security Authority later admitted they made a mistake and suggested he file a claim for the change fee he incurred.[6]

Think Like Steve

As in Steve Jobs. As you innovate and drive change in your operation, some of the best ideas people come up with will be for brand new products, services, or processes an organization has not tried before. Keep in mind that markets that do not exist cannot generally be analyzed effectively, and often, customers like things the way they are now. Steve Jobs and Apple rarely asked a customer what they thought of an idea, or waited for complete market or other information before proceeding with a product. Apple told people what they were getting, and the market adjusted.

We can't always wait for complete information before proceeding. If you understand your customers and the organization is aligned with their interests, an agile firm will proceed and new markets will be created.

Stay in Synch with Change with an Eyes-Wide-Open Approach

Vending machine company Cantaloupe Systems worked with Jasper Technologies to build the first "smart" vending machines, as part of a 100,000-machine network across the United States. The machines now provide feedback to employees with inventory levels, as well as monitoring customer preference in real-time, local temperatures (higher temperatures lead to peak beverage demand and lower consumption of chocolate or salty snacks), and even theft and vandalism activity with onboard cameras.[7] Supply and restocking operations are now simplified and improved significantly.

What information do you receive on a daily basis? Is it aligned with strategy? Does it facilitate timely problem resolution? Is the organizational data machine in synch with strategy? If culture is the embodiment of our behavior, your actions as a leader with this data will enable you to begin to shift the firm's collective behavior. How do you react to the information? What questions do you ask? Who do you talk to, and where do you focus?

While we are considering the data and other information you have at your disposal on a daily basis, be aware that that data will often get worse before you see an improvement as a result of your agility efforts. Lean advocates agree that their efforts often result in reductions in inventory or safety stock, increased operating capacity, or a requirement for less floor space. Performance metrics in these situations will drop, as stale inventory is written off or operations are idled as orders catch up with inventory. In fact, most performance measurement metrics will be based on "old" or legacy model behavior, rather than your new approach. My advice here is to talk to your controller ahead of time and keep the finance and accounting people in the loop; the initial numbers have derailed many such efforts as leadership was unable to see through the pain and keep the goals and objectives locked in.

Stop Blaming Your Culture

I cannot tell you how many times I have heard an executive lament, "That won't work here; we don't have that kind of culture." I will not disagree that whatever tactic or strategy we are discussing may not work *right now*, but that is hardly a reasonable excuse for not considering the idea.

This is an important point—the objective of these ideas is not a wholesale improvement in your culture; it is the recognition that we change our culture through the implementation of processes, tactics, behaviors, and ideas. An improved and agile culture will be an outcome of what you do next as leaders in your firms. Culture is not a separate component of your business, to be blamed when things go off the rails; we need to resist the idea of not doing something important because it does not seem to fit our idea of who we are right now.

Beware the Bias

Think back for a moment on the one last story that wrapped up Chapter 7 regarding the young couple looking for their GoPro camera in the Caribbean. Our perception of what happened in that case shifted quickly once we had more information. Further, our own biases and opinions led us to one conclusion based on the information we had at the time, however incorrect that conclusion was.

We all have biases, beliefs, and opinions that are a result of our education (formal or otherwise), environment, upbringing, social circles, religious beliefs, and experience. Many of those biases will lead us astray if given the opportunity. My intent here is only to remind us of the existence of biases and that our planning, communication, and execution need to account for and appreciate some of those biases. Overconfidence and optimism have sullied many a plan or project, and hindsight bias can give one the impression that we really know what happened. We have all been told that we may not be as smart as we think we are. Humility is our friend in many change situations.

Move Your Chair

Where you sit and work obviously has a large impact on who you interact with. Think about the challenges or strategies in front of the organization today, and then who you and others would spend more time with in the interest of driving those goals.

Would we benefit if research and development (R&D) and marketing colocated?[8] How much more customer-centric would our research be if we had current market and customer information? Would operations have a better appreciation for customer needs if their leadership shared space with sales? Would sales be better able to communicate what the organization could commit to if they worked more closely with operations? Would information technology (IT) and operations benefit by cohabitating during the implementation of a new enterprise resource planning (ERP) platform?

These can be temporary moves, intended to facilitate a change or initiative important to the organization. The premise is to facilitate dialogue and problem solving in the interest of executing a strategy.

Know When You Are at Your Best

Back in our Lean discussions, I asked what you would do with an extra hour every week. This section is similar in that it is about personal and organizational performance, and when the best time to get work done is around the organization. There are many studies out there, but most agree that we are at our most productive early to midmorning, and at our least engaged midafternoon.[9]

Many of us appreciate this already, so why do we tackle our email inbox or schedule less important meetings in the morning? Some of this is a time zone effect—those in the far east or west often need to alter behavior or schedules to accommodate colleagues on the other coast. Fair enough. For the rest of us, however, encourage your team to do the important stuff in the morning, keep any meetings in that period brief, and even encourage people to ignore their email for a few hours.* Productivity, and an appreciation of what really matters around the firm, will increase as a result.

That is my culture buffet; take what you like or what serves your purpose, and leave the rest behind. There is no one-size-fits-all approach to aligning people's behavior with the goals and objectives of the firm; the key is that you do not let your existing culture stop you, and take action in some way to create that alignment. The output of this approach will be both improved insight and appropriate action within the organization.

One insight you may gain is that the "rules" of the organization, the way you have worked in the past, will no longer apply. Change agents have been breaking rules for centuries. Wal-Mart rewrote the rules associated with supply chain management in retail. Many of you are familiar already with tactics and methods applied by the chain, but supply chain strategy was what really set Wal-Mart apart from other retailers in that space. Sam Walton once called the CEO of Proctor & Gamble (P&G) and asked him to come to Bentonville, Arkansas, for a meeting. The P&G man paused for a moment, and Sam said again, "You had better come. I have something really important to talk to you about."

The CEO arrived, and Sam Walton pointed out that Wal-Mart accounted for more of P&G's business than the whole country of Japan, yet P&G did not have offices or representation in Bentonville like they did in Tokyo and other parts of Japan (including R&D facilities). Walton told the CEO that this was going to change if they were going to keep doing business together, and it did. Wal-Mart's behavior with its supply chain community changed the historical dynamic and took the traditional power away from these suppliers, giving the influence to Wal-Mart.[10]

Steve Jobs took a similar approach, often putting suppliers into a particular business to accomplish his goals and objectives. A classic case comes from the birth of the iPhone. Jobs did not want a plastic screen on the device, preferring the feel of glass. During the development of the phone, he called Corning Glass and said, "Let me speak to your CEO." When the two eventually connected, Steve outlined his needs. Wendell Weeks, then-CEO of Corning, indicated they had worked on a product called Gorilla Glass, which was scratch resistant and had ion transfer to support a touch screen, and Jobs indicated that was what he wanted. Weeks said they had

---

* I have been pushing this idea for years with various organizations. It's a sad reflection on today's society that email takes priority over work that adds value. More on this in Appendix A.

never actually made it, but Jobs told him how much he needed, and that Apple needed the glass by September. With Weeks's mouth hanging open, Steve told him, "Don't be afraid. You can do it."[10] The rest is history, as they say, and Gorilla Glass became a staple of iPhones and iPads, as well as creating a whole business unit for Corning, cementing its focus on new products and an agile R&D culture.

Jobs and Walton had the ability to do that. They were imaginative, creative in their own ways, and refused to look at the current state as the best state. Most importantly, they forced others around them to see things differently and to align their work to support that new vision. People like Sam Walton and Steve Jobs were catalysts, and the concept of a catalyst is the last area of focus in our discussion of driving an agile culture.

What is a catalyst? Think back to your high school or university chemistry class for a moment. You will recall that a catalyst is something that facilitates a reaction that may otherwise not take place. That catalyst may be another chemical we add to the beaker or flask, causing something to happen. The reaction may require heat, a spark or motion (stirring or shaking), or sometimes both, but the catalyst enables and facilitates a desired reaction or outcome.

What are the catalysts that drive change in your business? When asked, executives often respond with economic conditions as a catalyst, such as currency exchange rates, interest rates, or the price of oil. These conditions, or the events that drive them, can be catalysts for change, but as often as not, they are actually anticatalysts, provoking a firm to stall or stand still if the change is in the "wrong" direction. Oil and gas investment and exploration essentially ground to a halt through 2015 as oil prices plunged to record low prices; the oil pricing event in this case caused organizations to halt any action and shut down strategic projects.

Competitor strategies and actions can stimulate change, as long as our own biases discussed earlier do not create a "we know better" mindset, as we saw with Blockbuster earlier in the book. The problem here is that a reaction to a competitor's initiative may be more aligned with the competition than what customers really want, so tread lightly in this area. Crises or catastrophes are obviously catalysts, and while the adage says, "Never waste a good crisis," we can't control or create a crisis as part of most strategies. Collectively, then, these external catalysts cannot form the foundation for change within our firm; they may be misaligned with customer need, delay action, or be too random to rely on.

The most appropriate and effective catalyst for most of our organizations is a person, an individual within the firm who has the ability to create a vision, help others see that vision, and align us all so we are moving together in a particular direction. Who is that catalyst within your organization? Could it be you? Without some spark to get us moving, some event, condition, or person that gets us out of our chairs, all the other work we have done here may be for not. People need and rely on leadership.

Figure 8.4 outlines what I call the "three legs of change," and the concept here is simple. Whatever capabilities we build as an organization, even with a change-driven culture, for the campaign to really "stick," we need a champion, a cause, or a catalyst to get us moving. The proverbial stool tips over without it. At the same time, we should appreciate some of the anti-catalytic forces around us, those things that act as barriers and cultural

FIGURE 8.4
The three legs of change.

anchors, invoking inertia and preventing us from doing the right thing and moving in the best direction for the firm. Here are some examples of those cultural anchors:

- Hierarchy and organizational structure. Firms like Borders and Research In Motion knew the appropriate next steps, but could not navigate fast enough to execute. President Obama's decision to appoint a White House staffer to lead the implementation of the Affordable Care Act (ObamaCare) was a structure decision, despite urgings from capable outsiders, and led to the mediocre launch of the program.[5,11]
- Rules, procedures, or policy. These act like a legacy effect, leftovers from the way we used to work, and can take years to work out of your organization. As an example, the Bank of Canada discontinued the $2 bill in 1996, and a decade later, there were still more than 100 million of them in circulation.*
- Collaboration overload. While the output and impact of collaboration is usually very positive for an organization, the effort and time required to maintain it add up very quickly. Think about how much time people around the firm spend in meetings, conference calls, or even email. Some data indicates those activities add up to 80% of people's time.[12] Over the years, I have team-taught a number of courses at the university. Team teaching is always more work per individual than simply taking a course and dividing the work by the number of professors responsible. Although the quality of the product is enhanced, the administration does not recognize or appreciate that effort, resulting in fewer professors being willing to team up.

Consider and be aware of cultural anchors like these, but never let your culture be an excuse for not doing the right thing. Your legacy is just that— old news. A good example of this is within the province of Alberta, and more specifically, the city of Calgary. Alberta has long been an energy-based economy, with vast resources in oil and gas. Those resources kept Alberta among the most well-off provinces in the country for decades, enabling an environment with no sales tax at the provincial level and supporting continued infrastructure spending that was the envy of all Canadians.

---

* Pennies were also sacked by the Bank of Canada a couple of years ago, and it seems these will disappear more quickly. I used a couple the other day to round out my change at a grocery store and the clerk was shocked, having forgotten already how to deal with exact change.

Conditions have changed, however. Oil prices have plummeted, gas prices are stagnant, and the province has been mired in a recession for a number of years. While oil prices will likely rebound, environmental pressure on emissions and an oil-based economy will only increase, forcing political leaders to consider alternatives and a movement toward a new provincial strategy. Part of the plan in Calgary is to build a foundation on low-carbon energy initiatives and support investment in other technologies and business areas.

Initiatives on the table include investments in renewables and clean technology, transportation and logistics, and agribusiness. Calgary recently opened a film studio, capitalizing on the success of the movie industry in Toronto and Vancouver. The city is looking for ways to facilitate start-ups and microbusinesses, knowing that a few of these will be future stars of industry. The city could wait it out, and bank on the return of the oil economy, but it is choosing not to.[13]

What are your customers buying? Our general answer throughout the book has been *execution*. Your customers are buying your execution, your ability as an organization to get things done and make things happen in alignment with your customers' needs. For an airline, and in fact a manufacturer of aircraft, that execution manifests itself in the provision of seats—seats at the lowest cost, going to the right destination as quickly as possible and as comfortably as is reasonable.*

Boeing is one of the world's dominant aircraft manufacturers, supporting military, commercial, and private aviation, along with a substantial space program. Over the past 50 years, it has done a very good job of satisfying its clients in these distinct markets, with a number of iconic and very recognizable aircraft, including the 747 (the first wide-body passenger jet and largest-capacity commercial plane on the market for almost 40 years) and the 737 (the most prolific design of all time, and staple of airlines such as Southwest and WestJet). While it struggles with new product launches, like all aircraft companies, Boeing has survived many commercial competitors over the decades, and now effectively shares the passenger market with Europe's Airbus.

Such was not always the case. Through the 1930s and 1940s, Boeing was seen as a builder of military aircraft first and commercial aircraft second,

---

* We could add in our personal preferences, including leg room, boarding priority, decent and affordable food, movies, and entertainment, but I will table that dialogue in the interest of expediency.

having got its start with the U.S. government. This was not necessarily a bad thing. Air travel was still relatively new, and primarily the domain of the well-off in society. World War II and other military campaigns were a priority, and in fact, those efforts funded much R&D for organizations like Boeing that eventually led to new commercial aircraft. During that period, however, Boeing's passenger aircraft were really just redesigned planes based on military platforms, and the airlines of the time realized this. As a result, Boeing often lost orders to firms like Douglas, which were seen as more customer-centric by United Airlines and Pan Am. Even its physical location in Seattle was a barrier compared with Douglas's headquarters in Los Angeles.

A number of things changed for Boeing in the early 1950s. A softening in military spending and the loss of several airline contracts led to financial struggles. The evolution of the jet engine provided design possibilities that could speed travel and reduce costs to the point of opening up commercial markets to a much wider group of customers. Boeing also benefited from a strong advocate within its customer ranks, and collectively, these circumstances helped Boeing lead the airline business into the jet age.

Determined to take a more customer-centric approach, Boeing pitched early concepts for its first passenger jet, the iconic 707, to Pan Am's CEO Juan Trippe. The potential range, speed, and cost per seat-mile* all immediately captured Trippe's attention. Trippe assigned his number two, John Borger, to work with and effectively push Boeing and keep it on track with the aircraft.

The 707 design evolved, sometimes due to input from Borger, often as a result of engineering and design (this being Boeing's first passenger jet, much was new), and even in reaction to information on early competitor products (the 707's two rows of three seats was in reaction to Douglas's DC8 design with a similar seating configuration). Eventually, the 707 launched, becoming the most popular passenger jet of its time, outselling the DC8 by almost 2:1† and cementing a customer-centric mentality within Boeing. Although Boeing would sometimes convert passenger aircraft for military purposes (versions of the 707 and later the 767 were converted as airborne refueling tankers), it never again tried to sell an airline a converted military design.

---

* One measure of an airline's productivity is its cost to fly one seat 1 mile.
† Boeing sold 1010 707s to Douglas's 556 DC8s.

ONE LAST STORY

In a recent behavioral experiment, a group called The Fun Theory (an initiative of Volkswagen) analyzed why people continued to avoid the stairs in public locations, and take escalators or elevators, even in a society where we are more and more health conscious than at any time in the past. As part of the experiment, the group observed commuters exiting a subway station at Odenplan, in Stockholm, Sweden, where the passengers had a choice between an escalator and a wide set of stairs. Cameras recorded most people choosing the escalator while the staircase remained virtually empty.

The group's hypothesis in the experiment was that they could change people's behavior if they made the activity interesting or fun. To test the hypothesis, they converted the staircase to an operational musical keyboard, an inclined "piano," complete with both white and black keys, generating music over nearby speakers.* As people climbed the steps, the appropriate musical note played when their feet touched a stair.

When the subway station opened the next day, people initially headed for the escalator, as their ingrained behavioral impulse dictated. On seeing the adjacent piano, however, many detoured to see what was up. When stepping up the stairs, the commuters were accompanied by music of their own creation. Cameras tracked their behavior over several days, and the experiment recorded an increase in stair traffic of 66%, including a number of elderly or mobility-challenged individuals who could obviously benefit by riding the escalator.

Countries like Norway and Denmark enjoy more electric vehicles per capita than any other country in the world, despite the fact that neither country actually builds any cars, let alone an electric vehicle. Their government achieves this carbon-friendly behavior by incentivizing drivers with free tolls, free parking, and subsidized charging for electric cars, while gas-burning vehicles pay full fees. Purchases of electrics cars qualify for healthy rebates from the government as well.

An organization's culture is just the representation of its behavior at a point in time. Culture itself is without thought, and absent of accountability; it can't be blamed in the event of poor execution. Culture can be bent, molded, shaped, and enhanced. It can be aligned to suit your purposes

---

* See the experiment on YouTube: "Piano Stairs – TheFunTheory.com."

and enable the attainment of those grand opportunities, the next big thing for your firm. A catalyst will be required, however, to lead that first step; will that be you?

REFERENCES

1. Asimov, I. *Robots and Empire*. New York: Doubleday Books, 1985.
2. Barton, C. The introverted corporation. BCG Perspectives, April 27, 2016.
3. Murray, A. Lessons from the Fortune 500. *Fortune*, June 15, 2016, p. 14.
4. Katzenbach, J.R., Steffen, I., and Kronley, C. Culture change that sticks. *Harvard Business Review*, July–August 2012.
5. Kotter, J. *XLR8: Accelerate*. Brighton, MA: Harvard Business Press, 2014, pp. 4, 58.
6. Graveland, B. Airport screening agency sorry for refusing to pat down man. *Globe and Mail*, August 20, 2015, p. A7.
7. Shoot, B. The smart vending machine. *Fortune*, November 17, 2014, p. 49.
8. Harnish, V. 5 ways to shake up your offices. *Fortune*, February 1, 2015.
9. Bellini, J. Apparently this matters: The worst time of day for work. CNN.com, June 8, 2013.
10. Serwer, A. Steve Jobs vs. Sam Walton: The tale of the tape. *Fortune*, December 3, 2012, p. 128.
11. Karlgaard, R. Team management: Think small and agile. *Forbes*, December 2, 2013, p. 32.
12. Cross, R., Rebele, R., and Grant, A. Collaboration overload. *Harvard Business Review*, January–February 2016, p. 76.
13. McIntyre, C. Naheed Nenshi on how Calgary can thrive in a low-carbon future. *Canadian Business*, June 21, 2016.

9

Simple Closure

Simple applies everywhere.

I won't keep you much longer.

The central theme of this book is a focus on speed and agility, and in fact, competing with urgency and an understanding of who our customers are and what they want. Agile organizations garner greater customer enthusiasm, while wasting less time and energy in areas where value is not created. Through our discussion over the previous eight chapters, we can hopefully agree that *simple* and Lean apply everywhere within our firms.

In Chapter 4, I referred to a study by Bain and Company, where an apparent disconnect was highlighted between service organizations and their target market. The study found that the leadership at some 80% of organizations believed their firms provided superior service to their customers, while only 8% of customers of those organizations indicated that they received superior service. We can appreciate how a service provider may believe they provide superior service—no organization is in business with a goal of mediocrity. Given our own experience with many of these providers, however, how can the gap (80% vs. 8%) be so large? That is, how do so many managers and owners believe they are doing a great job when their customers are collectively left frustrated?

I believe there are a number of reasons for this, but at its core, it comes down to alignment. We applied the concept of alignment early in the book, as we sought to better understand our customers, and as part of our A^3 change realization model (Figure 9.1) introduced in Chapter 5 in the pursuit of aligning internal resources toward the organization's goals and strategy. Here, we will conclude the discussion with another look externally, and the alignment of the organization with the needs of its

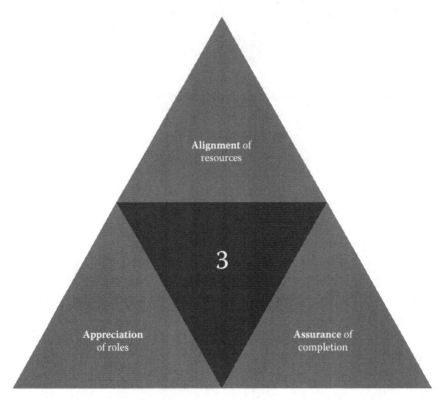

FIGURE 9.1
A^3 change realization model.

customer. The firms that mistakenly believe they are providing superior service do not know their customers. It really is that simple. They have not taken the time to understand who their most important customers are, and especially what that group of people want or need from the service. That lack of alignment externally ensures the lack of alignment internally, where the firm's strategy, resources, and operations are not driven toward ensuring customer satisfaction.

I relied on the customer definitions provided by Gregory Stone in 1954 earlier in the book, where we all embody either personalizing, ethical, economizing, or convenience behaviors as customers, depending on the situation. Stone's terms were a great place to start as we began to think in more depth about our customers, and then how we would operationalize our product or service delivery accordingly. How much time do you spend thinking about your customer? Do your processes and services align to support those customers?

The fast casual restaurant market evolved because there were customers who would pay for, say, a really good hamburger, but didn't want to sit through the traditional restaurant experience or compromise with fast food. In this case, the restaurateur would need to focus on both the quality and type of ingredients and operationalize an expedient, consistent preparation system.

Let's quickly revisit a few of the central tenants and themes within the book.

- **Agile strategy:** The key for you here is to know your customer. Every organization has one, so what does your customer want, and what don't they want? Spend more energy developing a vision for the firm that creates value for those customers, and less time doing other things. That is, an effective strategy is what you will do, while at the same time articulating what you are not going to do.

  While the strategic planning process should never be rushed, this clarity of focus enables your leadership team the license to allocate resources and create a roadmap more quickly, and pivot when necessary, moving the group in a new direction. The simpler message resulting from the strategy process is easier to both communicate and grasp by those in the organization responsible for its execution. And, as we have shown, your customers are buying your execution, and not much else.

- **Simple reflection:** What would you do with an extra 60 minutes every week? I was teaching an MBA class recently and the building's aging HVAC systems were struggling. That day, the classroom temperature soared to very uncomfortable levels, so I cut the class short by an hour, as much out of sympathy for the students as for myself sweating at the front of the room. The next day, the system was under control and the room was quite comfortable. I asked the students what they did with their free hour, having just talked Lean earlier in the week. There were lots of smiles, but no good answers.

  This obviously isn't a surprise among a group of students, but what about you and your organization? How do people react when time is freed up in their schedule? Do they have a clear list of priorities, tasks, and objectives focused on supporting the firm's goals? Time to goof off or unplug is essential, especially in a high-energy agile organization, but there should never be a sense of confusion or lack of clarity regarding what is next on the employee's agenda.

That same reflection and prioritization pushes people toward dealing with organizational scotoma, identifying process and structural issues within the firm, and dealing with anything that gets in the way of what matters most to their customers. Do it now!

- **Lean innovation:** In our scope, innovation applies to far more than just products. While that application is by far what people recognize most as innovation (e.g., new technology, features on their cars, electronics, and household goods), innovation is attainable for all of us, in the form of process, service, and even business model innovation. When we appreciate that broader perspective, we may acknowledge that many of our organizations are more creative and innovative than previously thought.

  At this point, it is important to be reminded of two key elements of an innovative culture: First, maintain a healthy sense of paranoia. Look over your shoulder and check your blind spots. How is the industry changing? What policy shift could threaten us? How are customers behaving differently within our realm? If we ceased to exist as a business tomorrow, would anyone notice? Be wary of plateaus, and don't wait for economic conditions to be ideal—they never will be. Pivot boldly, and minimize your innovation gap between business models and their related cycles.

  Second, look for base hits too. Start with a dysfunctional process in the receiving area or a bottleneck in the customer's application process. Cancel a regularly scheduled meeting or report that creates little value. Get a fresh pair of eyes to walk through your operations with you, looking for issues the team has been blinded to. This is the firm's execution—you own it, and customers want it.

- **Agile culture:** Your culture is the output of the collective behavior within the firm, yet it is often thought of as an input, and blamed for poor results and failed execution. Stop blaming your culture, and correct the behavior. Align work toward goals and objectives, help the team appreciate how their work impacts the customer and supports the firm's strategy, and then follow-up, achieving the assurance that we are working to plan. Stay focused on agility and serving the customer, and you won't go wrong.

  The ability to shift behavior and get to an agile culture almost always requires a catalyst, some spark or change to act as the thin edge of the wedge. Don't wait for ideal government actions or competitive threats—let that catalyst be you. The following "One Last Story" section gives an example.

ONE LAST STORY

Russell Redenbaugh[1] graduated first in his class from the University of Utah in 1967. From there, he applied to several MBA programs, but was denied by the likes of Harvard and Stanford. Undeterred, Redenbaugh flew to Philadelphia and appealed in person to the administration at Wharton, was accepted, and graduated sixth in the class two years later.

Job offers were limited for Redenbaugh, despite his academic credentials, but he eventually landed with a Philadelphia investment firm as an analyst. By 1980, he was its chief investment officer and full partner. He left a full-time role with the firm behind a decade later, yet retained ties as he pursued government service and philanthropic objectives.

Looking for something more physically challenging, he began to study jiu jitsu at the age of 50, working with many of the masters of the sport despite his age. In 2003, Redenbaugh traveled to Brazil to compete in the Jiu Jitsu World Championships, where he competed in the master's senior-level competition. He won gold. He returned in 2004 and 2005, and won gold in his class again both times.

What you don't know yet is that Russell's hobby as a teenager was building model rockets. At the age of 16, a rocket he was assembling blew up in his hands, removing a number of fingers, and eventually blinding him in both eyes. While in the hospital recovering from the injuries and related surgery, he determined that this event would not be a handicap, and would not prevent him from succeeding in a "sighted" world. Everything he accomplished, including both university degrees, his business success, and especially on the jiu jitsu mat, was against fully sighted and nonhandicapped opponents.

They say that 80% of success is showing up. What are you doing with the other 20%?

REFERENCE

1. Karlgaard, R. True grit: Blinded and gifted. *Forbes*, September 23, 2013.

Appendix A: Communication II: Email and Making Sense in the English Language (Abandon All Hope Ye Who Enter Here)

Query to a listing we placed in Kijiji: "Is the item still available?"
"Yes it is," I reply, yet I receive no further response from the above party. Were they just checking?

What shouldn't be simple? Your email password.
(But sure, write it down!)

It is possible that some of you may look at this addendum to the book and feel it may not quite fit the overall theme. The book, after all, is about agility and eliminating complexity within the organization to get things done. We have discussed communication, and the importance of getting our message heard, with a priority on aligning resources around the firm toward our goals and objectives. That all makes sense, so why revisit the topic?

Good question! (They told me you were smart, dear reader.) The key challenge we look at here is at a more granular level, the basics and fundamentals associated with some of our primary forms of communication. This includes email and some of the terms, phrases, idioms, and metaphors we use to connect and ideally increase comprehension with our audience. Terms like *granular*. What the heck does that even mean in this context? Is it small, like sand or sugar? Is there a difference between grains of wheat and barley? I think it means getting down to a more fundamental level, to the core or foundation of the problem or challenge at hand, right? Then why not say that in the first place? How about these?

- Sorry, but I will be *out of pocket* at that time. Translation: Not available. Again, why not say, not available? I heard this one for the first time on a conference call with some folks from GM. *Wait*, I thought, *did he use to play football?* The not-so-subtle secondary meaning is that the individual using the phrase doesn't think you need to know what they are really doing at the time of your event.
- *Back in five* (a note you stick on your door). Innocent enough, and intended to be helpful. My friend Keith, whose office is down the hall, kindly pointed out that unless someone saw me leave my office, they would not know if I had left almost five minutes ago and will return soon, or had just left, and they needed to wait at least another five minutes. Hmm…. As a result, I stopped putting up the notes, not wanting to confuse anyone. No one was looking for me anyway.
- *Ass over teakettle.* Our kids rolled on the floor laughing when Grandma used this phrase recently. I could not find the origin online, but it refers to one taking a spectacular tumble of some kind.
- I wanted to *reach out* to you. This one is used most often in email conversation when someone seems to want to ask you a favor. The phrase always sounded a bit odd to me, but perhaps I am being peevish. Use it cautiously, however; when one sees *reach out* on an email, someone wants something. One may stop reading.

There is now an endless supply of these phrases, euphemisms, and substitutions. Some are quite stylish, reminding us of the sophistication of the speaker, while others merely confuse. The challenge is that our brains often turn our ears off and we stop listening when one of these phrases is inserted into the dialogue we were listening to. *Wait, what did she say?*

Some people are just smarter than I am, and speak that way, which is fine. See Bill Belichick's address to the media in Chapter 7, or notably the conversation between Neo and the architect in the *Matrix: Revolution* movie. If the purpose of our communication in a business environment, however, is to inform, align, negotiate, motivate, or perhaps investigate, there is no room for misunderstanding or confusion. *Simple*, in the context of this book, needs to apply also to our language and core message. Dumb it down so people know what you are talking about.

Sometimes it is not our turn of phrase, but the way the English language is constructed. How is it that we can repeat the same word in a sentence and it makes sense? Example: *The audience had had enough.* There is some sort of past-tense possessive going on here, but we understand it. How much of our brain capacity is taken up understanding all of these little rules and idiosyncrasies of our language? The word *that* is another that can be strung together a couple times. How about *there, they're,* and *their,* or *two, too,* and *to*? Madness.

This is admittedly a bit of a goofy discussion, but the purpose is to highlight how easy it is for us to lose a listener (or reader, for that matter—are you still there?).* Used effectively, our language is an incredible tool. It is such a fine line, however, between the appropriate construction of a message and the frowns and befuddlement that result when reasonable care has not been taken. Sadly, the inception and integration of email into our lives has only made it worse.

Here are some statistics:

- A McKinsey study indicates we spend a third of our workweek managing email.[1] Another study has the number at 28%, which could still amount to a modest number of 40 emails per day, or 10,000 per year.[2]
- Three-quarters of all email is unnecessary or junk,[3] much of which is unfortunately not blocked by our systems (not the fault of our information technology [IT] people; nefarious senders get more creative every day). We therefore waste uncountable hours dealing with the inbox rather than on productive work.
- Workers spend 111 workdays every year dealing with email.[3]

These numbers are staggering, although sadly not surprising. Email has become so much a part of our lives because it is essentially free, universal, and easy. Few organizations manage the practice of email within their firms either, by default giving managers and employees permission to continue with a lack of structure regarding email communication. Even if we ignore for a moment the time and wasted resources associated with managing email,† the practice of email itself is flawed. It is far too easy to be misunderstood, or for people to send a potentially inflammatory message electronically.

Email messages are essentially one-dimensional; they are just the words. There is no emotion, facial expression, or tone of voice to provide emphasis or inflection in support of that message, so people often misunderstand the

---

* My secondary purpose is to satisfy my editor, who asked for 60,000 words on the book and I was a little short.

† I appreciate that this suggests that one-third of email is productive. That same math results in at least 80 workdays per year wasted on unnecessary or unproductive electronic communication. What could you do with an extra two weeks every year?

intent of our words. Thankfully, some of our best and brightest in society have created priority symbols (!) and emoticons to lend emotion or clarity to a poor communication system. Still, have you sent a tough or provocative email and been anxious about the response when you see a reply in your inbox? How much more effective would this discussion be in person?

Email will not go away, and sadly, it will be waiting for you when you return from vacation (for those of you strong enough to ignore your email while on vacation). Perhaps we will evolve, although I am skeptical. With that in mind, as organizational leaders, we need to appreciate and acknowledge the disruptive nature of email, and manage our communication more effectively. Our goals should remain focused on the core purposes of our communication: to inform, educate, align, negotiate, or investigate. As such, there needs to be a more natural ebb and flow associated with that communication and an assurance that our people get the information they need when they need it.

We know that having our work interrupted by a phone call or email disrupts our cognitive capabilities for up to 25 minutes.[4]* That is, following one of these interruptions, it can take us far longer than we appreciate to return to previous levels of performance. A goal, then, should be to reduce the number of these interruptions we subject ourselves and our employees to on a daily basis. A secondary goal should be to increase the accountability of our communication, where email depersonalizes or removes some of the implied responsibility of that communication. Ultimately, if email isn't going away anytime soon, how do we make it, and our overall approach to communication, more effective?

Verne Harnish, CEO of Gazelles Inc., writes a column for *Fortune* magazine, often providing bullet "how-to" ideas for improving one element of your business or another. He suggests these five ways to liberate[5] your team from some of the email challenges noted above:

1. Don't try to solve problems by email; get the team together in person.
2. Make subject lines more specific. This increases comprehension and attention.
3. Insist on brevity; keep it simple.
4. Ban emails with multiple parts; one theme per message.
5. Close the conversation quickly. If that is not possible, see number 1.

---

* There is also a study I refer to often by King's College at London University that indicates that email lowers your IQ. Search "Email lowers IQ" for references.

These are all good ideas, and I like the way Verne thinks. Do you talk to your team about email, best practices, guidelines, and when to step away from the computer and go and talk to someone in person. Think back to the Toyota Production System and TPS Principle 12—*Go and see.* This absolutely applies here.

Treat email like the productivity killer that it is, and apply a Lean methodology in dealing with it. Reduce the overproduction and defects associated with email, the unnecessary "Reply all" usage or CC (carbon copy) of notes to people who really do not need to be part of that conversation. Am I creating value with this message, or am I merely adding to the gridlock that is our email traffic jam within the firm?

Another approach I have used, and recommended to numerous organizations, is to give people permission to ignore their email. This sounds a bit odd, but many of our employees are placing an inappropriate level of priority on electronic communication. In fact, some studies indicate that our self-worth or self-esteem increases with the number of emails we receive on a daily basis, so we subconsciously allow the process to manage us and enable it to grow. We need to step away and manage email, not the other way around.

The way this works is to start by giving people a couple of hours per day when they are permitted to ignore email. Even further, mute the device, don't take it to meetings, and create a small period in the day when there are no interruptions. Start this process a single day per week. Those two hours are now your time—focus on that priority we have discussed or something else of interest to you. Gradually add in more days in the week until people recognize that, say, between 1 p.m. and 3 p.m. is our "email-free zone." I have had many executives report back that once they got everyone to see that they were serious about this initiative, those two hours became the most productive of the day. It even shifted people's behavior and the culture of the firm away from being managed by email to focusing on the core priorities of the business. People became more creative, productive, and agile.

Organizations that have applied some of these tools have seen a reduction in email traffic by as much as 64%, and a resulting gain of up to 10,400 man-hours, or a 7% increase in productivity.[6] Any other tactic or approach in gaining this type of productivity would require significant time and capital investment in most organizations. What would you do with that time around your firm? How would you apply that available capacity if you could free it up?

ONE LAST STORY

Katrina and I were in an Irish pub in Manhattan recently, and imagine my delight when the sign on our table indicated there was a St. Patrick's Day special of a shot of Irish whiskey and a stout beer for about $8. When the server came by, a sweetheart with a lovely Irish accent, I ordered the special.

She asked, "So, are you Canadian?"

We smiled, and I asked, "How did you know? I didn't say 'eh' even once!"

She said, "It's the way you said 'stout.' It sounded like 'stoot.'" I have heard that we as Canadians pronounce some words differently than our friends south of the border—process and 'praw-cess,' about and 'a-boot.' We are less aware of the differences in pronunciation than our listeners obviously are, but in this case, I was called out (most politely) by an Irish woman in a New York restaurant. Perhaps, even in a global environment, we are better understood and appreciated than we think.

REFERENCES

1. Rao, L. Email: Unloved, unbreakable. *Fortune Magazine*, May 1, 2015, p. 54.
2. Email is broken. *Canadian Business*, March 2015, p. 54.
3. Gill, B. Email: Not dead, evolving. *Harvard Business Review*, June 2013, p. 32.
4. Sergut, G., and Gunther McGrath, R. Managing under complexity: Where is Einstein when you really need him? *Ivey Business Journal*, May/June 2010.
5. Harnish, V. Five ways to liberate your team from email overload. *Fortune*, June 16, 2014, p. 52.
6. Brown, C. To reduce email, start at the top. *Harvard Business Review*, September 2013, p. 26.

Appendix B: East Coast Historical Society Operating Plan

This appendix is an abridged example of an operating plan from our friends at East Coast Historical Society (ECHS) and, more specifically, the introduction of their Thanksgiving supper event in the fall.

Figure B.1 illustrates the two-page version of their operating plan. This abridged version outlines the work associated with the new launch, and does not include other operating projects for this year or work planned at other divisions. It does provide a sense of how we map out those key projects, and then how those projects will serve the greater good within ECHS. The full operating plan for an organization like ECHS might run 12 or 15 pages.

In this case, I have illustrated specific financials associated with the event, including one-time capital expenditures and period expenses, plus an estimate of first-time sales the team believes they can capture in 2018. The projects themselves include facilities, marketing, and the recruiting and training of the team executing the event in the fall, highlighted because we haven't run something like this before in that season. Also broken out in this example is a small section for notes after each project. At each operating plan meeting, the various stakeholders within ECHS can make notes on their copy of the operating plan, ensuring continuity throughout the project.

Opening Remarks: East Coast Historical Society (ECHS) will evolve to a year-round business model, developing products and services that augment its existing attractions, appealing to both historical enthusiasts and new guests.

Company Goals:
- Develop new attractions in typically off-season months.
- Leverage new leadership tactics and implement an agile business model, focusing on the creation of customer value while eliminating work the customer would not pay for.
- Achieve a level of financial independence enabling the society to create a new model for historical tourism operations.

Divisional Targets Early Settlers Division:
1. On-time launch of the Thanksgiving supper event

Financial Summary:
Early Settlers Division (selected numbers, this fiscal year):

Thanksgiving facilities (one-time investment)	$260,000
Marketing for new Thanksgiving event	$20,000
Case member recruiting and training	$30,000
Case member compensation, Thanksgiving event	$160,000
Food and preparations	$140,000
Projected guests, Thanksgiving, 12,000 at $40 each	$480,000

Key Operating Indicators:
@ Jan 1:   Website hits, monthly visits, conversions of one-time tickets to membership
@ Dec 31:   Same metrics; measures impact of project launch

Projects in This Plan:

Project description: Thanksgiving facilities
Develop a floor plan for the Thanksgiving event within the courtyard, including tables, staging, and an open area for dancing. Project includes the acquisition of any necessary period-appropriate fixtures and furnishings to support the event.

Project lead:	Events director, ECHS
Target completion:	August 31, 2018
Project budget:	$260,000

Notes:

FIGURE B.1
ECHS operating plan (abridged).   *(Continued)*

Project description: Case member training
This project includes the recruiting of any new staff and training of the team associated with running the Thanksgiving supper event, including food preparations, serving, and especially entertainment during the event itself. The project does not include compensation or benefits during the event.

Project lead:	Operations director, ECHS
Target completion:	September 30, 2018
Project budget:	$30,000

Notes:

Project description: Thanksgiving marketing
As this is a new event, this project will build the awareness and enthusiasm for the Thanksgiving project. Activities include local promotion, social media, and appeal to long-term members and advocates for ECHS activities.

Project lead:	Marketing director, ECHS
Target completion:	September 30, 2018
Project budget:	$20,000

Notes:

Rollout Plan:
Townhall meeting planned for June 15, this fiscal year. Speaker: CEO.
Internal supporting communications and team meetings commence late June.
Responsibility: Early Settlers Division directors.Reinforced through continual review and monitoring of the operating plan and support of project gate reviews.

FIGURE B.1 (CONTINUED)
ECHS operating plan (abridged).

Appendix C: Personal Lean

The more you do something, the easier it gets,
making it all the harder to stop doing.

Ralph Waldo Emerson

Even a correct decision is wrong when it was taken too late.

Lee Iacocca

This appendix is devoted to you, your individual activities within and
without the firm. The way you organize your work, how you interact, and
how you shape that behavior to influence others. Establish your priorities,
and then work on finding more time to focus on the things you wish to
spend that valuable time on.

I included an appendix on personal Lean in my first book, *Lean Innovation*.
Have a look there as well if the topic interests you. I am not repeating that
work here, but augmenting it, demonstrating that the more time you spend
with an idea, the more you learn about it.

We have all thought, *I wish I had more time*, often in the context of
spending more time doing what we are doing now, be it a key initiative,
solving a problem, spending time with family or friends, or extending that
well-deserved vacation. That is an important statement, but really just the
first, small step in the direction of freeing up time. Furthering the thought,
I have two questions for you: (1) How can you have the time if you do not
take the time? (2) What would you do with that time if you had another
hour (or more) every week? I have asked you the second question before,
so hopefully you have written down the answer.

I will preface this by saying I am not a lifestyle coach or self-help guru;
that is not what we are about here. I have found, however, that we can
apply the Lean concepts and philosophies typically targeted at our firm
and its operations to our own behavior. This is where we will focus here.
Like the "culture buffet" discussed in Chapter 8, this is a similar approach,
laid out on a table where you can take and work with the personal Lean

tactics you like or believe fit your needs, and leave the others behind. I would also encourage you to come back later to this section and pick up another tactic to try around the organization. These are not new ideas for the most part, but in our complex, digital world, I have found we need to work even harder to avoid distractions, focus, and get the right work done.

DO IT ONCE

Look around your desk. Somewhere there is a file or folder you have looked at a half-dozen times, thought about it, maybe even made some notes, and then put it back down again. Many people have a number of such files on their desk, files that we even move numerous times to find another file we want to work on right now.

Do your best to just touch the file once. Deal with the problem or situation at that time; don't keep moving the work around your desk, burying it, only to find it again a week later and mumble, "Oh yeah, I have to deal with this." Some options for that file?

- Delegate: Give it to someone who needs the work, could benefit from exposure to this kind of work, or is better qualified to do the work well. Hand it off to your minions.
- Delete: Admit that perhaps you may not do this at all. That is OK. The fact that the file somehow made it to your desk is not your fault. Give it a pass, give it back to the sender indicating the time is not right for this [insert word here]. Say no; if you can't say *no*, you can't manage your time.
- Deal with it: Yep, do it now. Having exhausted the options for delegate and delete, this may need to be done by you, so let's get on with it.

EXECUTE A PROPER HANDOFF

In many cases, the work we struggle with has not been assigned effectively, but dumped on our desk in a "drive-by" manner, with minimal instruction or clarity, but with a goal or deadline attached (recall the "poor instruction" within the paper airplane exercise). While some responsibility falls to the recipient to ask for clarity, the delegator generally bears the burden of fault in poor handoffs. What we know now is that we will have to spend less cumulative time as managers on a particular task we have delegated if we spend a bit more time up front executing proper delegation.[1]

- Connect the work to the firm's strategy and direction. Employees will understand the priority you are placing on the work, and how it connects to their jobs.
- Keep it manageable. Don't hand off too much at once, especially to newer employees. How do you eat an elephant? One bite at a time.
- Insist on clarity. Employees and team members will not read your mind; that is the sole responsibility of your spouse. Make sure expectations have been clearly expressed, and that the recipient understands the expectations, including content, due date, and format.
- Thank you. Express gratitude, and perhaps congratulate someone who does an exceptional job with the task. Courtesy never goes out of style.

BEWARE OF EXCESS MULTITASKING

Some people wear multitasking like a badge: "Pile it on, I can take it!" While it is difficult and sometimes impossible to not be involved in a number of projects at the same time, we know that multitasking can have a number of negative effects on our work and the organization itself if left unchecked. The quality of work may be diminished, and stress and anxiety increase in individuals trying to juggle multiple initiatives at the same time, especially when priorities are not clear or timelines overlap. In our context here, the quantity of work completed decreases, often attributed to the ramp-up time associated with starting a new task.

In two separate studies, output was measured and compared between work groups, where one group was given free reign and multiple assignments, and the other group was more tightly managed and focused on fewer objectives. In the first study, knowledge workers on computers were tracked over the course of a number of days. The first workers managed one task at a time, completed it, and moved on. The second workers had multiple assignments and self-managed. The outcome was that the first workers completed more work and were productive 85% of the time, while the second workers were measured to be productive only 33% of the time.[2]

In the second study, a group of Italian judges were randomly assigned cases and were measured on the number of cases they closed over a course of months. The judges who were assigned fewer cases at a time actually closed more total cases than judges with larger portfolios. Further, judges with fewer cases on their dockets took less time per case.[3]

Multitasking behaves like traffic; the more cars we put on the road, the longer it takes to get to the destination. The paradox is that to get more done, and free up our time, we need to have less work occupying our limited focus at any one time.

FOCUS

Stating we should limit or reduce our multitasking is one thing, but how we achieve that state of nirvana is another. Our distractions are too numerous to list, but as my sister Cheryl likes to say, we are all distracted by shiny objects, including our phones, email (see Appendix A), people knocking on our doors, and even unnecessary meetings on our schedule. It is up to you to jealously guard your schedule, and protect the time you have to get what you want done. Some of you will have a pit bull executive assistant who helps with that work, but it is ultimately up to you how you spend your time. Here are some thoughts to get you started:

- Turn off the ringers. Including email audible tones, vibrations, or other noises. If it is important, they will track you down. Otherwise, the text or email can wait until you choose to stop what you are working on. Turn off the office monitor with CNN or the stock market on it and focus.
- Ditch the open-door policy.[4] Sure, leave it open when you can, but when you really need to get some work done, close the door and let people know you are busy. I have seen some people use a green–yellow–red approach, where green is *come in*, yellow is *intrude if you really need to*, and red is *touch the door and I will beat you with a stick*.

- Review your meetings. Look at the list of recurring meetings on your calendar, and rank that list from most valuable to wasting your time. Kill the meetings at the bottom, or work with the owner or sponsor of those meetings to help them add value. Insist on meeting protocol, such as publishing agendas ahead of time, no smartphones, and people showing up on time.

GET SOME SLEEP

It is well documented that digital devices at night can disrupt your sleep, especially when viewed right before you turn out the lights, as a result of the color spectrum and intensity of the light itself. E-readers are better, but can still have an impact.[4] If your tablet or phone is your device of choice, there are special glasses you can use to reduce the effects of that light, but better yet, go old school and pick up a book or magazine. Let your brain unplug, and you will sleep better, making the next day more productive.

STOP BUYING STORAGE

Buying more storage products, such as hard drives, cloud space, or physical storage like a filing cabinet, Rubbermaid tote, or even filing boxes, should not be necessary unless you are growing your business. Even then, think twice about adding space: What can I eliminate first? What files can I delete or shred? That PowerPoint from 2009 will never be reviewed again. What totes can I empty in the storage room, basement, or garage? That stuff has been there for years! On a personal note, for every new item of clothing you buy, try donating one old piece; you probably haven't worn that item in a couple of years anyway. Clean out your fridge.

There are a lot of tactics like this; you all have one approach or another that makes you more effective and efficient. We need such methods just to keep ahead of the alligators nipping at our heels both personally and professionally. My goal with this discussion is simply timeliness, the outcome of doing the right thing at the right time. As we become better at managing our time, we will have more of it to work with.

At first, you will struggle with that free time, looking for something to fill it. That is perfectly natural. You know what, though? It is also OK to procrastinate; you have earned it.

REFERENCES

1. Schachter, H. Lighten your load with a proper handoff. *Globe and Mail*, October 15, 2012, p. B5.
2. Harvard Business Review Staff. The multitasking paradox. *Harvard Business Review*, March 2013, p. 30.
3. Mangelsdorf, M. How too much multitasking at work can slow you down. *MIT Sloan Management Review*, Spring 2011, p. 96.
4. Harnish, V. Five ways to get organized. *Fortune*, September 1, 2014, p. 42.

Index

Page numbers followed by f and t indicate figures and tables, respectively.

About the Author

Barry Cross joined Queen's University, Kingston, Ontario, Canada, in 2006 after spending a number of years in industry. Barry is now an instructor, consultant, and speaker with the Smith School of Business in operations strategy, where he works with students and diverse organizations in areas of strategy, Lean, innovation, projects, and execution. He has an MBA from Queen's University, has published numerous articles, and is the best-selling author of three books, including *Lean Innovation*, *Project Leadership*, and *Simple*. He lives in Belleville, Ontario, Canada.